MEL BAY'S
GETTING INTO.........
GUITAR IMPROVISING
A SYSTEMATIC APPROACH TO SOLOING

by

SCOTT REED

Contents

CD Contents

1 Example 4 [1:11]	12 Example 36 [1:30]	23 Example 72 [1:14]	33 Example 111 [:49]
2 Example 11 [:45]	13 Example 40 [1:27]	24 Example 77 [1:23]	34 Example 113 [1:12]
3 Example 12 [:42]	14 Example 44 [:47]	25 Example 80 [:37]	35 Example 115 [1:10]
4 Example 14 [:44]	15 Example 45 [:49]	26 Example 83 [:38]	36 Example 117 [:49]
5 Example 15 [:44]	16 Example 46 [1:29]	27 Example 87 [1:27]	37 Example 118 [1:05]
6 Example 17 [1:22]	17 Example 50 [:43]	28 Example 89 [1:23]	38 Example 121 [1:03]
7 Example 20 [1:52]	18 Example 51 [:49]	29 Example 97 [:48]	39 Example 122 [1:37]
8 Example 22 [:42]	19 Example 56 [1:17]	30 Example 99 [:49]	40 Example 123 [1:24]
9 Example 23 [:44]	20 Example 60 [1:27]	31 Example 109 [:41]	41 Example 144 [:59]
10 Example 26 [2:18]	21 Example 65 [:45]	32 Example 110 [1:16]	42 Example 155 [2:55]
11 Example 30 [1:28]	22 Example 70 [:42]		

Foreword

The material in this method is designed to apply to any style of music.
The integrated approach of this method will;

1. Introduce and cultivate an understanding of the theory behind improvisation.
2. Provide ear training through musical examples.
3. Promote better visualization of shapes on the fingerboard through diagrams.

This book is intended for the guitarist who has longed to learn the art of Contemporary Improvisation, but has been unable to find a method that combines the theory with musical examples and a practical approach to the guitar fingerboard.

The musical examples in this book can be played with both a "swing" eighth feel and a straight eighth note feel to make them adaptable to various musical styles.

Swing Eighths:

Played as:

Symbols and Techniques

B = Bend - bending or pushing the string up to the note indicated.

RB = Release Bend - releasing a note bent up in pitch to the original fretted pitch.

S = Slide - sliding along the string into the pitch indicated.

H = Hammer-On - "hammering on" one of the left hand fingers to produce the note.

P = Pull-Off - pulling off the fretted finger to a note already held down with a left hand finger to produce the note.

HP = Hammer-Pull - this technique involves three notes. The initial note is picked with the right hand, the second note is "hammered-on" with a left hand finger, and the third note is "pulled-off" with that same left hand finger.

↓ = Down Pick

↑ = Up Pick

3

Understanding the Modes

The first basic step in the study of contemporary improvisation is to gain an understanding of chord scales or "modes" (as they are often referred to). The best way to understand how they work is to look at the relationship of the major scale and its relative minor scale. It's called "relative" because the minor scale has the same notes as it's related major scale except that it <u>starts on the sixth degree of that major scale</u>.

Ex. 1

You can see that if you start on the sixth degree of the C major scale (the note A), and continue for one octave you get an A minor scale. To take this concept a step further, you could start on any one of the seven different degrees of a major scale and essentially get seven different scales. This is how the modes are derived. They are named **Ionian** or major for the first degree, **Dorian** (2nd degree), **Phrygian** (3rd), **Lydian** (4th), **Mixolydian** (5th), **Aeolian** or natural minor (6th), **Locrian** (7th), and of course **Ionian** again for the octave (ex. 2). You can use this process for building the modes in any key simply by starting on the first degree of the major scale and building one octave scales on each degree of the major scale.

Ex. 2

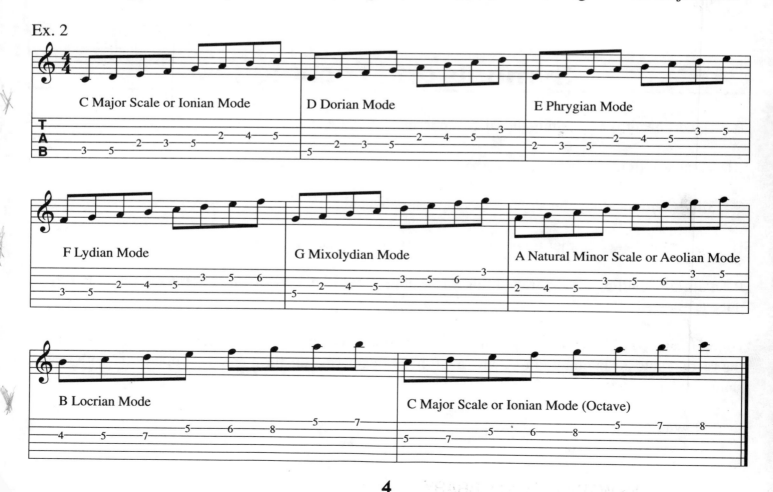

In order to visualize how building the modes relates to the fingerboard, let's take a major scale form you may be familiar with - the G major scale in the second position with the root on the second string (ex. 3).

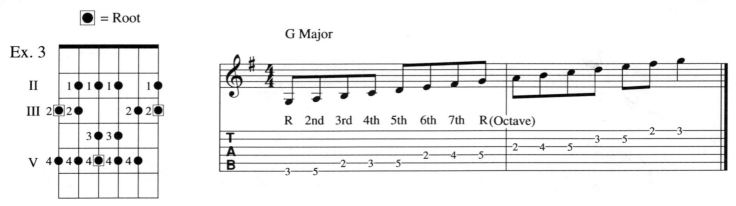

You of course can play a one octave scale from G to G which would be the Ionian mode or major scale. Now if you start on the note "A" (the second degree), and play a one octave scale (from A to A), you would have an A Dorian mode. By starting on each of the remaining scale degrees and playing one octave scales, you will derive the rest of the modes in the key of G major (ex. 4).

Diagrams for Example 4

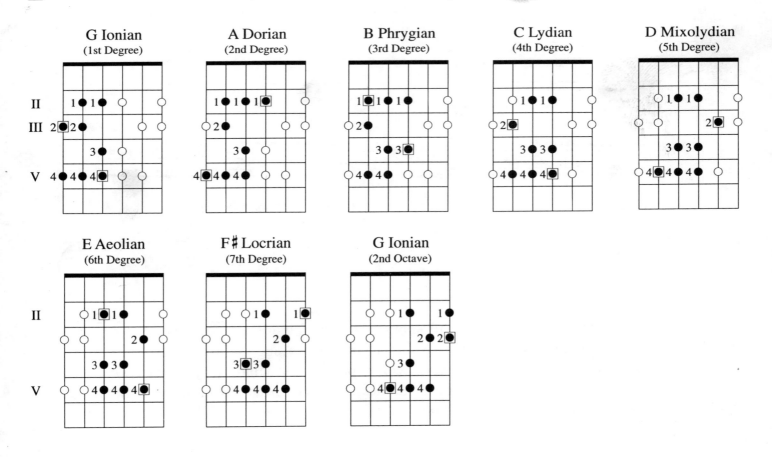

Ex. 4

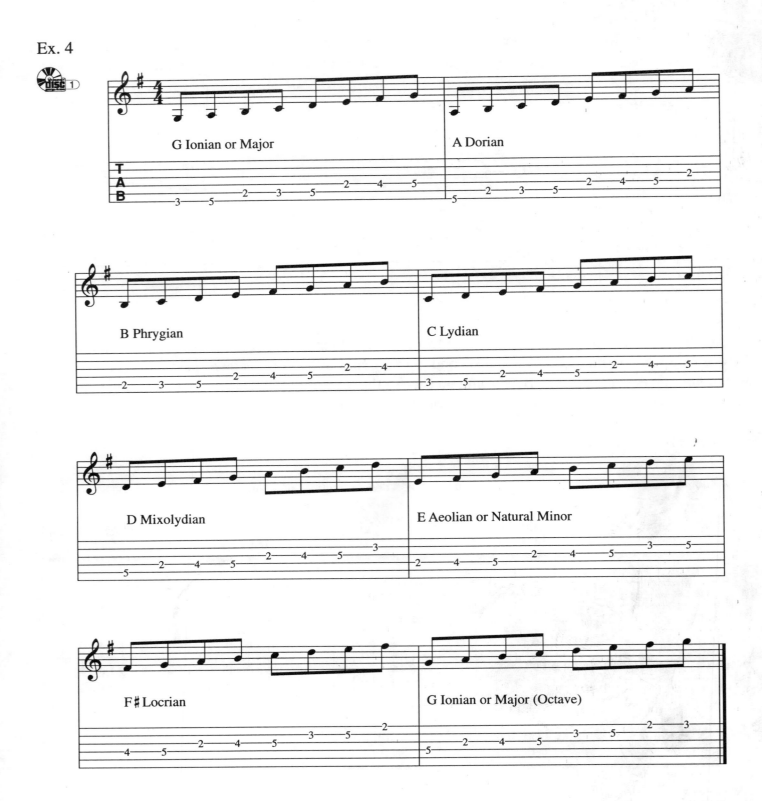

It is important to explore the modes in different areas of the fingerboard. Figure A shows diagrams for the modes built from the G major scale in different positions throughout the fingerboard. The second position forms introduced in example 4 have been expanded to include two octaves where possible. Notice that in each of the positions some of the modes will have forms that have two complete octaves, others one complete octave with additional notes occurring above and below the root notes.

Figure A - Diagrams for the Modes Built on the G Major Scale

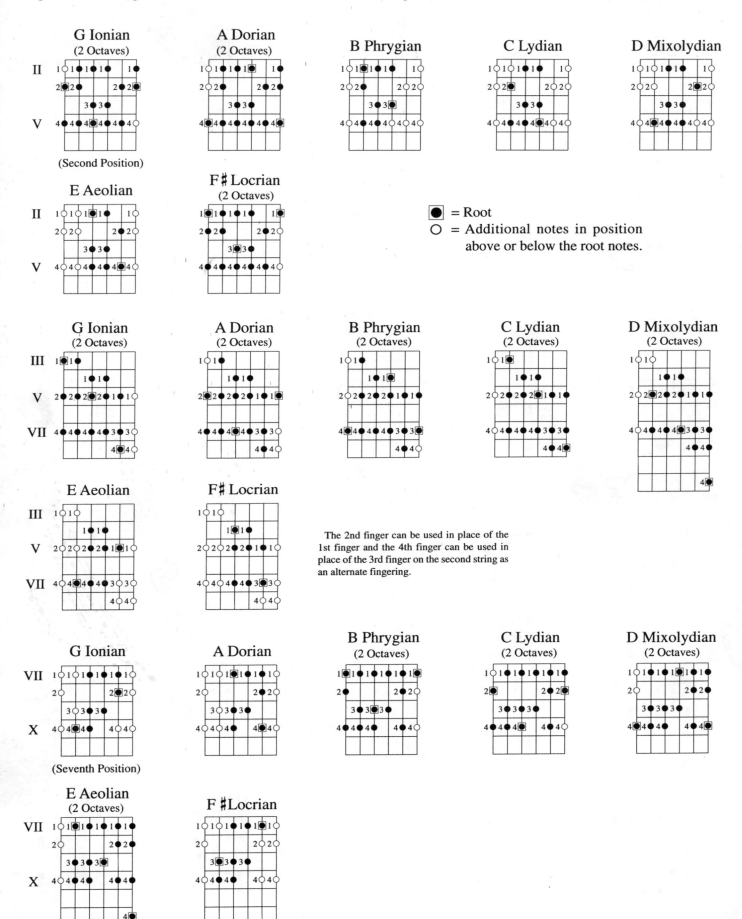

■ = Root
○ = Additional notes in position
above or below the root notes.

The 2nd finger can be used in place of the 1st finger and the 4th finger can be used in place of the 3rd finger on the second string as an alternate fingering.

Figure A - continued

G Ionian
IX
XII

(Ninth Position)

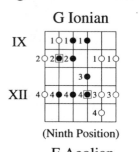

A Dorian

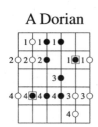

B Phrygian

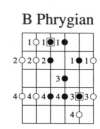

C Lydian

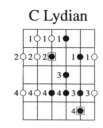

D Mixolydian
(2 Octaves)

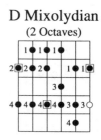

E Aeolian
(2 Octaves)
IX
XII

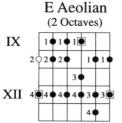

F♯ Locrian

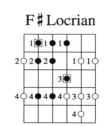

The 2nd finger can be used in place of the 1st finger and the 4th finger can be used in place of the 3rd finger on the second string as an alternate fingering.

G Ionian
(2 Octaves)
X
XIV

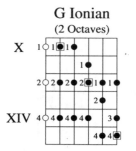

A Dorian

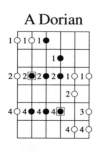

B Phrygian

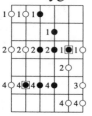

C Lydian

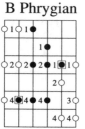

D Mixolydian
(2 Octaves)

E Aeolian
(2 Octaves)
X
XIV

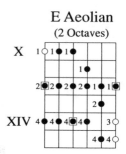

F♯ Locrian
(2 Octaves)

The 2nd finger can be used in place of the 1st finger on the second string as an alternate fingering.

G Ionian
(2 Octaves)
XII
XV

A Dorian
(2 Octaves)

(Twelfth Position)

B Phrygian

C Lydian

D Mixolydian

E Aeolian
(2 Octaves)
XII
XV

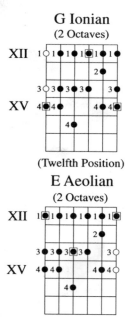

F♯ Locrian
(2 Octaves)

Alternate fingering for the 12th position

G Ionian
XII
XV

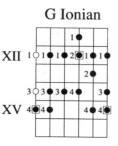

A Dorian

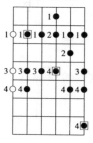

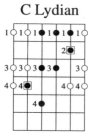

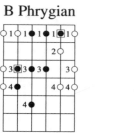

The notes on the third string can also be fingered 1 - 1 - 3 to accomodate different note patterns

8

Why They Are Called Chord Scales

Now that we have built modes on each degree of the major scale, it's time to look at building chords on each degree of the major scale. If you can understand that a Gmaj7 chord is built by stacking third intervals (using every "other" note in the G major scale) from the Root G, then it should not be surprising that this can be done for <u>each degree</u> of the G major scale. By using every other note (1st or root, 3rd, 5th, and 7th tone) from each of the modes built in the key of G major, we will derive chord tones for each degree of the G major scale (fig. B). These chords, are called diatonic chords, because they are built on each successive degree of the G major scale and all of the notes adhere to the G major key signature.

Figure B

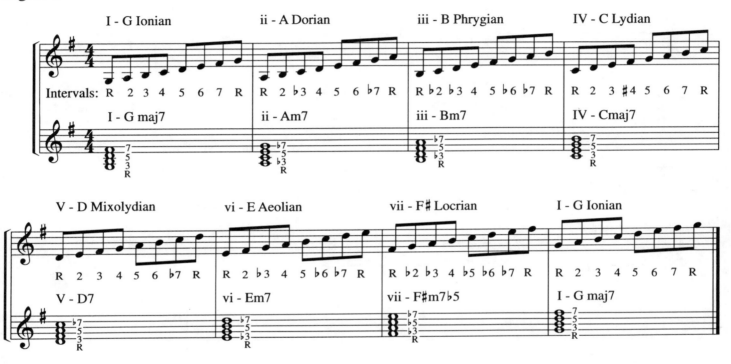

Since the guitar's voicings are sometimes different than a piano's (which might play the chord tones in order - root, third, fifth, seventh), example 5 shows chord voicings that are more easily played on the guitar.

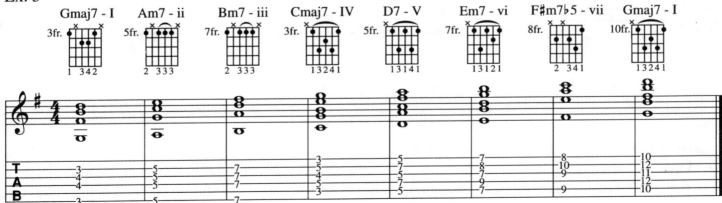

The roman numeral for the seventh chord built on the seventh degree of the major scale (vii) may sometimes be followed by the symbol "Ø", however the abbreviated form (vii) is used throughout this book.

The modes are called chord scales because each mode (or scale) has a corresponding chord that is associated with it (a pairing for each degree of the major scale). To get used to the sound of the chord and scale paired together, you should play the Gmaj7 chord and then play the G Ionian mode, then play the Am7 chord and the A Dorian mode, and continue so that you have played chord and mode for each degree of the G major scale (ex. 6). The chords in example 6 are voiced so that they are in close proximity to the G major scale form in the 2nd position.

Ex. 6

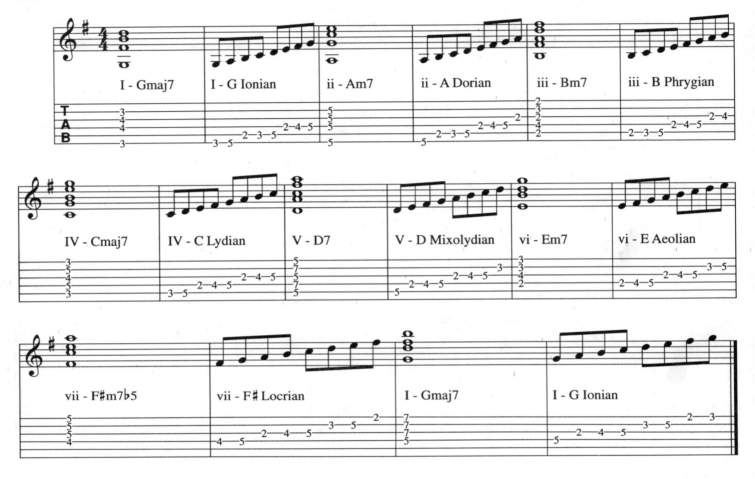

To break the monotony of playing modes in order, you can try different scale "patterns" as in example 7.

Ex. 7

Next you should try the chord-scale exercise in a way that might be found in the context of a song. In the key of G, you might see chord changes that follow a ii - V - I (Am7, D7, Gmaj7) pattern or a IV - V - I (Cmaj7, D7, Gmaj7) pattern. So, consequently, the chord-scale exercise should be done in this order (ex. 8). It is important to note that you can use "non-seventh" chord forms when matching chords with the modes built on the same major scale degree. For example, the Gmaj7 could simply be a G major chord (used with the G Ionian mode) or the Am7 could be an A minor chord (used with the A Dorian mode). This is important to remember when soloing over chord changes that don't have sevenths (Root, 3rd, 5th, only) or when playing over power chords (Root, 5th).

Ex. 8

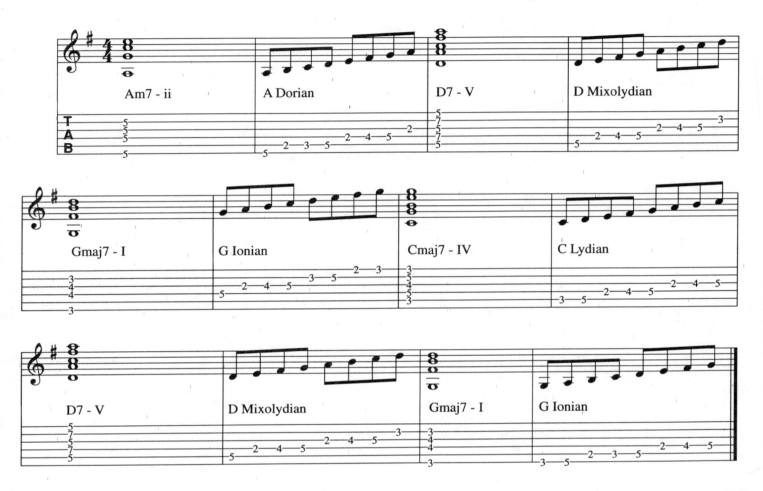

You should also try playing just the scales in the following order (ex. 9).

Ex. 9

11

When you get comfortable with this approach, you should try more difficult combinations such as iii - vi - ii - V - I (ex. 10).

Ex. 10

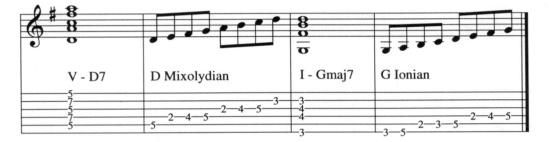

| iii - Bm7 | B Phrygian | vi - Em7 | E Aeolian | ii - Am7 | A Dorian |

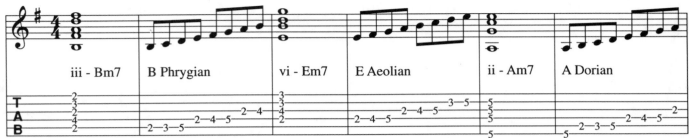

| V - D7 | D Mixolydian | I - Gmaj7 | G Ionian |

The following chord diagrams are included to provide additional voicings to go along with the chord-scale exercises in examples 6, 8, and 10. When paired with the scale shapes in figure A you will be able to play chord-scale combinations throughout the fingerboard.

Chord Forms with the Root on the 6th String

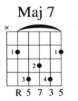

| Maj 7 | Dominant 7 | Minor 7 | Minor 7♭5 | Diminished 7 |
| R 7 3 5 | R ♭7 3 5 | R ♭7 ♭3 5 R | R ♭7 ♭3 ♭5 | R ♭♭7 ♭3 ♭5 |

Root on the 5th String

| Maj 7 | Dominant 7 | Minor 7 | Minor 7♭5 | Diminished 7 |
| R 5 7 3 5 | R 5 ♭7 3 5 | R 5 ♭7 ♭3 5 | R ♭5 ♭7 ♭3 | R ♭5 ♭♭7 ♭3 |

More Forms with a 5th String Root

| Maj 7 | Dominant 7 | Minor 7 |
| R 3 5 7 | R 3 ♭7 R | R ♭3 ♭7 R |

Root on the 4th String

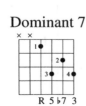

| Maj 7 | Dominant 7 | Minor 7 | Minor 7♭5 | Diminished 7 |
| R 5 7 3 | R 5 ♭7 3 | R 5 ♭7 ♭3 | R ♭5 ♭7 ♭3 | R ♭5 ♭♭7 ♭3 |

Musical Examples

Melodic Ideas Using Chord Patterns Derived from the Key of G Major

Ex. 11

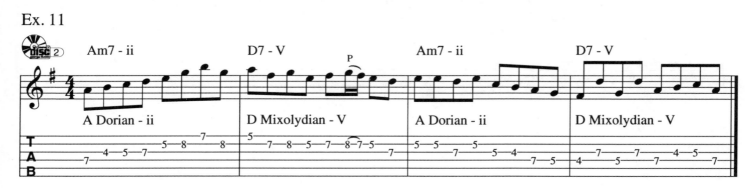

Ex. 12

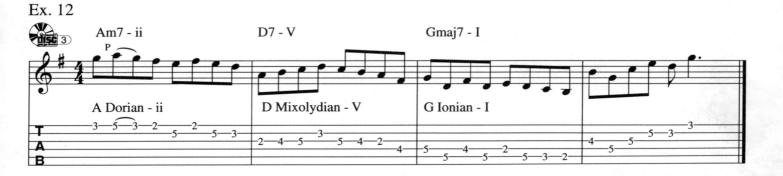

Ex. 13

Ex. 14 - Non-Seventh Chord Forms

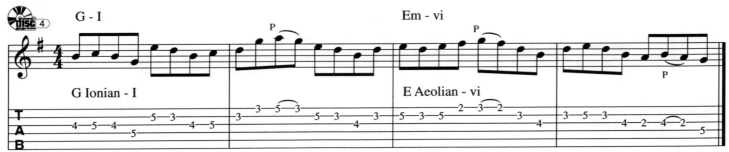

Ex. 15

Ex. 16

Ex. 17

Arpeggios or Chord Tones

The term arpeggio refers to a broken chord or chord tones that are not played together at the same time. For the arpeggios built in the key of G, you will use the same notes as shown before with the diatonic chords, but you will play them as an arpeggio (ex. 18). As with the diatonic chords, the arpeggios use the 1st (root), 3rd, 5th, and 7th scale notes from <u>each</u> of the modes. For basic non-seventh forms (root, 3rd, 5th, root), simply eliminate the 7th scale tone (or interval) which is the closest note below the top root note of the 7th arpeggio (fig. C).

Fingerings for the Arpeggios Built in G Major - Second Position
For diagrams with the arpeggio intervals see the Mode - Arpeggio guide at the end of the book.

● = Root   ○ = Additional arpeggio notes in position above or below the root notes.

Gmaj7 - I (2 Octaves)   Am7 - ii (2 Octaves)   Bm7 - iii   Cmaj7 - IV   D7 - V   Em7 - vi   F#m7b5 - vii (2 Octaves)

Ex. 18

Figure C - Non-Seventh Forms

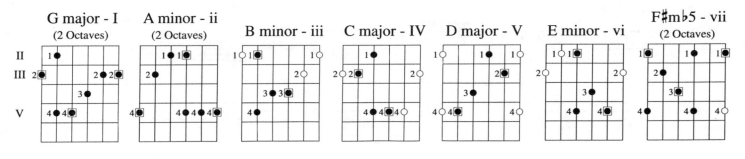

G major - I (2 Octaves)   A minor - ii (2 Octaves)   B minor - iii   C major - IV   D major - V   E minor - vi   F#mb5 - vii (2 Octaves)

A common technique used in modern soloing that involves arpeggios is the "brush" or sweep technique. The notes are organized so that the pick can "brush" across the strings, usually striking three or four strings with one down stroke or up stroke (ex. 19).

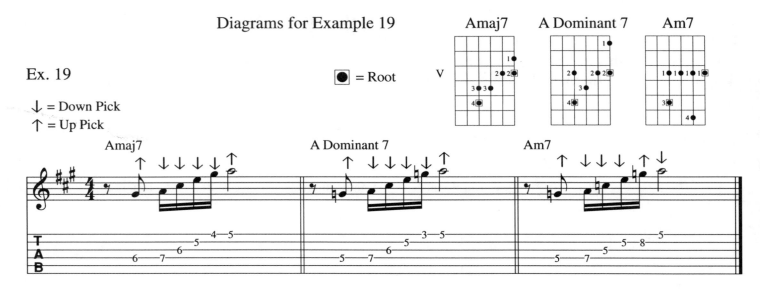

Example 20 pairs the arpeggios with the modes built off of each degree of the G major scale (in the same way chords and modes were paired in example 6). As with the scale forms shown before, the arpeggios can be played in many different areas of the fingerboard (fig. D) and correspond with the scale forms presented earlier. To see the arpeggios (and the arpeggio intervals) paired with the modes throughout the fingerboard, see the Mode - Arpeggio guide at the end of this book. For the different types of chords that go with the modes and arpeggios, refer to the Scale - Chord relationships chart at the end of this book.

Ex. 20

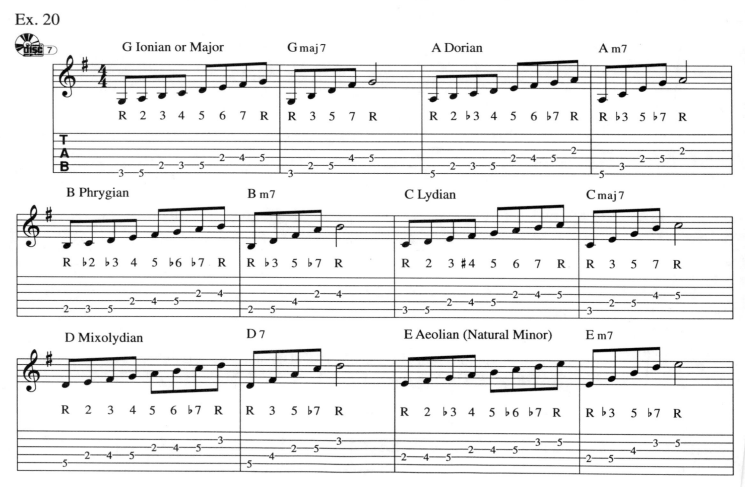

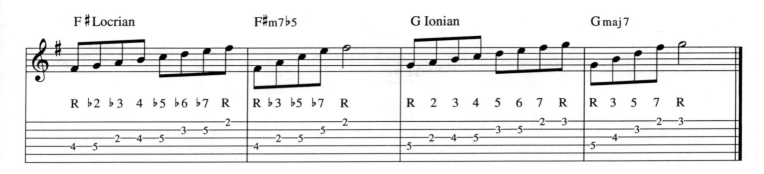

Figure D - Fingerings for the arpeggios built on each degree of the G major scale, positions III, VII, IX, X and XII. For the arpeggio intervals see the Mode-Arpeggio guide at the end of this book.

● = Root   O = Additional arpeggio notes above or below the root notes.

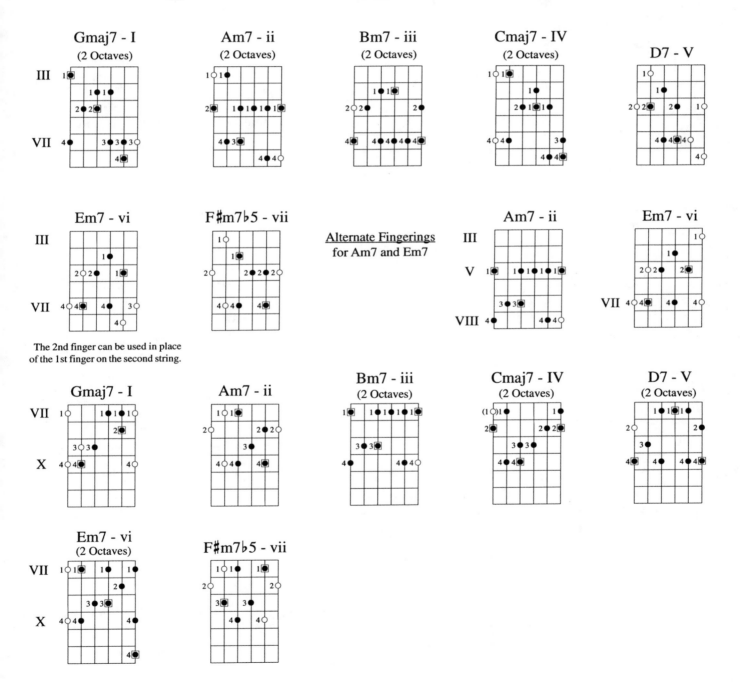

17

Figure D - continued

Gmaj7 - I
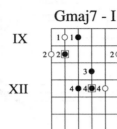

Am7 - ii
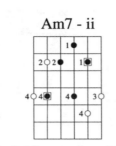

The 2nd finger can be used in place of the 1st finger on the 2nd string to accomodate different note patterns

Bm7 - iii
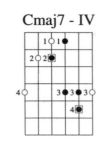

Cmaj7 - IV
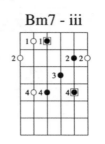

D7 - V
(2 Octaves)

Em7 - vi
(2 Octaves)
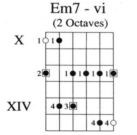

F#m7♭5 - vii
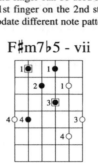

Alternate Fingering
for Am7

Am7 - ii
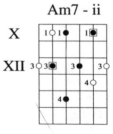

Gmaj7 - I
(2 Octaves)
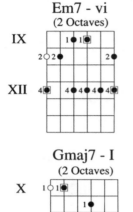

Am7 - ii
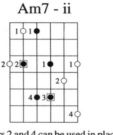

Fingers 2 and 4 can be used in place of fingers 1 and 3 on the 3rd string

Bm7 - iii
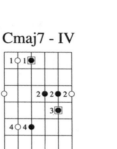

The 2nd finger can be used in place of the 1st finger on the 2nd string

Cmaj7 - IV

D7 - V
(2 Octaves)

Em7 - vi
(2 Octaves)
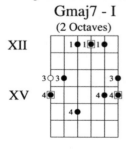

F#m7♭5 - vii
(2 Octaves)

Fingers 2 and 4 can be used in place of fingers 1 and 3 on the 4th string

Alternate Fingering
for Am7

Am7 - ii
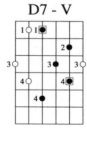

Gmaj7 - I
(2 Octaves)

Am7 - ii
(2 Octaves)

Bm7 - iii

Cmaj7 - IV

D7 - V

Em7 - vi
(2 Octaves)
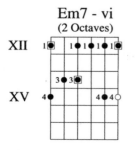

F#m7♭5 - vii
(2 Octaves)

Alternate Fingering
for F#m7♭5

Alternate fingering places the note F# on string 3 instead of string 4

F#m7♭5 - vii
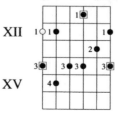

18

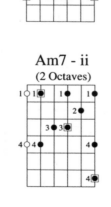

Probably the best way to reinforce these new forms is to play the arpeggio and scale together in succession as in example 20. This can be done for all the corresponding forms throughout the fingerboard. The examples have been given in the key of G, but since they are moveable forms they should be played in other keys and explored all over the fingerboard.

You can think of the chord tones as the "strong" tones that will reinforce the sound of the chord you are playing over. In Jazz this is often referred to as an "inside sound." By mixing the chord tones with the corresponding scale (or mode) you can create a feeling of tension and release (examples 21-24).

Ex. 21

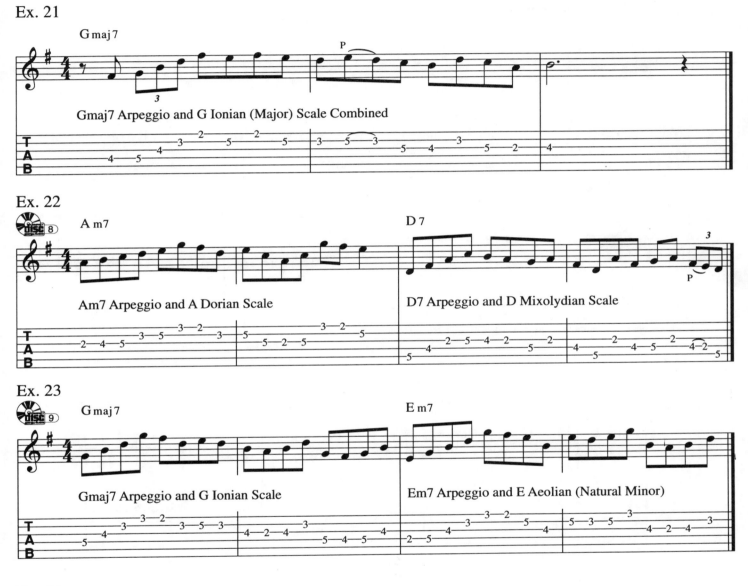

Ex. 22

Ex. 23

Ex. 24

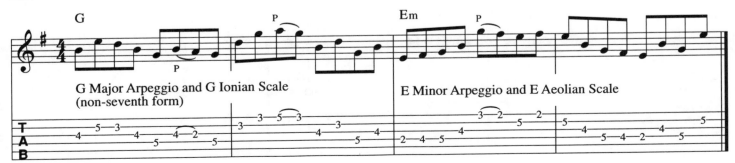

19

Pentatonic Scales

Using pentatonic scales in addition to modes and arpeggios can expand your melodic vocabulary. Notice in figure E that the G major and E minor pentatonic scales have the same notes. These are "relative" scales in the same way that the G major and E minor scales are relative because they contain the same notes, but the roots fall on different degrees.

Figure E - G Major and E Minor Pentatonics Compared

 = Root

G Major Pentatonic

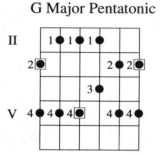

E Minor Pentatonic

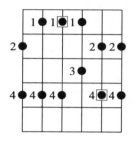

Fingers 1 & 3 can be used on the first and second strings in place of fingers 2 & 4 as an alternate fingering. In addition, the 2nd finger can be used on the third string in place of the third finger to accomodate different note patterns.

G Major Pentatonic   E Minor Pentatonic

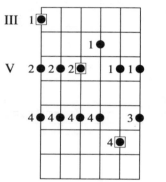

The 3rd finger can be used in place of the 4th finger on the third string as an alternate fingering.

G Major Pentatonic

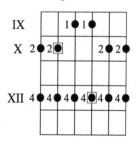

E Minor Pentatonic

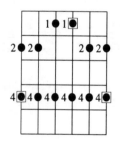

G Major Pentatonic

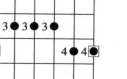

E Minor Pentatonic

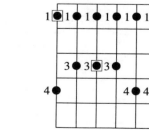

Ex. 25 - G Major and E Minor Pentatonics Compared

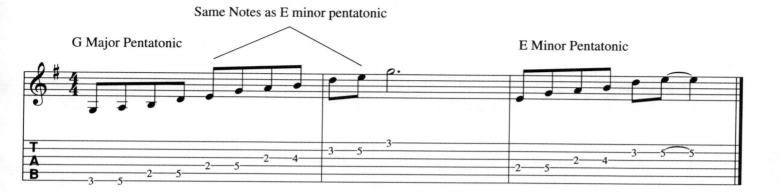

The following diagrams show how the pentatonic scale notes relate intervallically to the root notes.

G Major Pentatonic

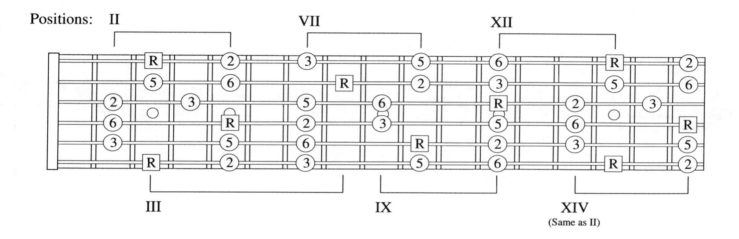

E Minor Pentatonic

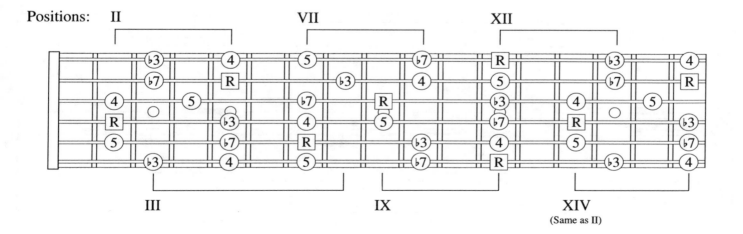

Example 26 combines the G major scale or Ionian mode (as well as the relative minor E Aeolian) with G major and E minor pentatonic scales and Gmaj7 and Em7 arpeggios.

Ex. 26

Incorporating Modes into Blues and Rock Improvising

You are probably aware of the frequent use of the pentatonic scale in Blues and Rock improvising. The principle here is that you're using a scale based on "one" root note through different chord changes as opposed to matching a scale (or mode) with each chord as seen earlier with the modes (this approach will be covered a little later). In order to incorporate a single mode into this style of improvising, we need to look at the mode which is closest (in terms of common notes) to the minor pentatonic scale. When comparing the various modes with the minor pentatonic scale, we find that the Dorian mode actually contains all of the notes in the minor pentatonic scale. The minor pentatonic scale has ♭3rd, 4th, 5th, and ♭7th, intervals above the root, while the Dorian mode contains these intervals plus a major 2nd and major 6th. The addition of the Dorian mode to this style of soloing can provide additional color when combined with the minor pentatonic scale over Blues or Rock chord changes. Because of the similarity of the blues scale to the minor pentatonic scale (the blues scale adds a ♭5 interval), the Dorian mode can also be used with the blues scale to create different melodic colors.

Since "mixing" the sound of the blues scale and Dorian mode can create some interesting colors, we can derive a "combination" scale that uses notes from both scales (ex. 28). You will find that many "classic" Rock and Blues licks use notes from this pattern.

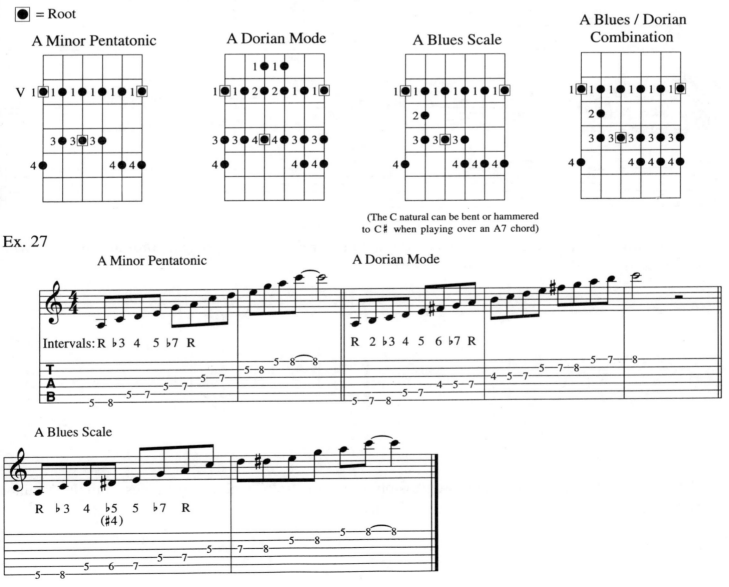

Ex. 27

Ex. 28

A Blues / Dorian Combination

Example 29 shows how the Blues, Dorian and combination scales can be used over a Rock or Blues chord progression.

Ex. 29

The chords in Example 29 (A5, D5, and E5) are often referred to as power chords and are built with only a root, fifth, and octave (no third interval).

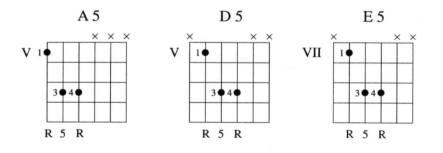

Example 30 shows a 12 bar Blues progression where the "solo" melody uses notes from the A minor pentatonic, A Blues, A Dorian, and A Blues / Dorian combination scales.

Ex. 30

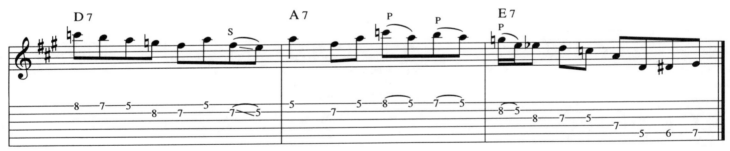

The A blues and A minor pentatonic scales contain the note C natural which is sometimes bent or hammered to a C sharp when playing over an A7 chord (C♯ is the 3rd of the chord). The C natural can also be changed to a C sharp when using the A Dorian mode in conjunction with the blues and pentatonic scales over an A7 chord (ex. 31).

Ex. 31

Expanding the Fingerboard

Because of the fact that certain licks lay better in certain areas of the fingerboard, it is important to know the blues scale and the minor pentatonic scale all over the fingerboard. Figure F shows the A minor pentatonic scale and the A blues scale in five positions along with diagrams for the whole fingerboard (note that the A blues scale is essentially an A minor pentatonic with a ♭5 interval added). You will find that alternate fingerings work in some cases to accommodate things such as bending, shifting to new positions or different note combinations. You should work on shifting in and out of positions so that these shapes become one scale. Notice, in the whole fingerboard diagrams, how the scale patterns in the different positions relate to each other along the fingerboard.

Figure F

A Minor Pentatonic Scale - 5 Positions

● = Root

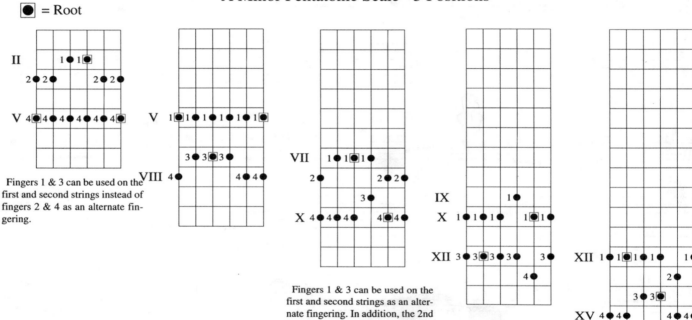

Fingers 1 & 3 can be used on the first and second strings instead of fingers 2 & 4 as an alternate fingering.

Fingers 1 & 3 can be used on the first and second strings as an alternate fingering. In addition, the 2nd finger can be used on the third string in place of the 3rd finger.

Whole Fingerboard Intervals

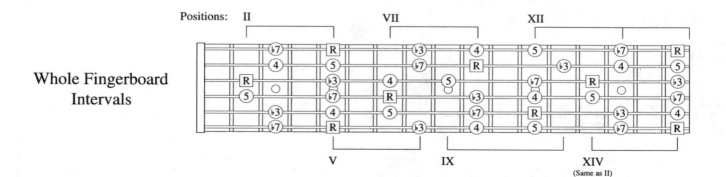

Figure F continued

A Blues Scale - 5 Positions

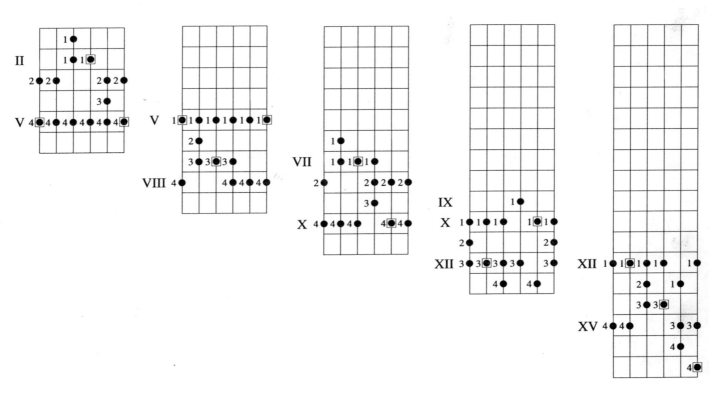

Whole Fingerboard Intervals

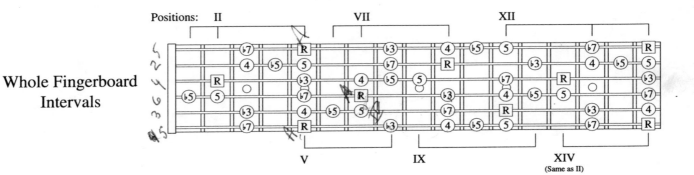

This page has been left blank to allow easier comparison to the previous diagrams.

Figure G shows alternate fingerings for the A Blues scale to facilitate different note patterns.

Figure G

A Blues Scale - (Alternate Fingerings)

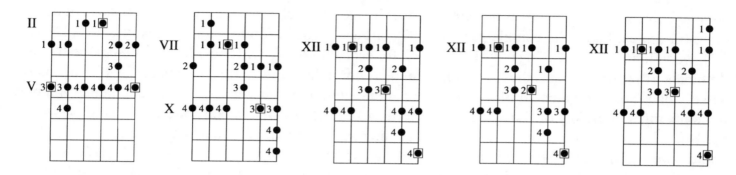

Example 32 illustrates the use of shifting positions with the A blues scale.

Ex. 32

Example 33 shows a lead pattern that links positions of the A minor pentatonic scale.

Ex. 33

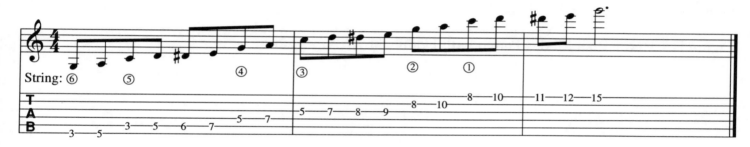

The Chord – Scale Approach

Changing the note C natural to C sharp (raising the third) actually turns the A Dorian mode into an A Mixolydian mode (which is the mode normally matched with a dominant 7th chord). This brings us to another approach to soloing over the Blues chord changes, the "chord-scale" approach. Instead of using a scale (or scales) based on a single root note ("A" Blues) through different chord changes (A7, D7, and E7), we will now look at using a different mode for each chord. We will use a Mixolydian mode for each dominant 7th chord because the Mixolydian mode is normally paired with a dominant 7th chord, and the Mixolydian mode contains all of the notes in a dominant 7th chord with the same root name (you may remember that in the key of G major the D7 chord had a D Mixolydian mode paired with it). If we look at the Blues chord changes from a chord and matching scale approach, because they are all dominant 7th chords, we will use an A Mixolydian mode for the A7 chord, a D Mixolydian mode for the D7 chord, and an E Mixolydian mode for the E7 chord. You will find that bending up to or sliding into the "3rd" degree of the Mixolydian mode adds more of a characteristic Blues sound.

Figure H pairs the A, D, and E Mixolydian modes with dominant 7th arpeggios (ex. 34). Example 35 shows how the use of dominant 7th arpeggios with the Mixolydian modes can accentuate the sound of the chord tones of the chords in the progression.

Figure H - Mixolydian Modes Paired with Dominant 7th Arpeggios

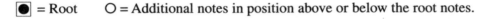

● = Root   ○ = Additional notes in position above or below the root notes.

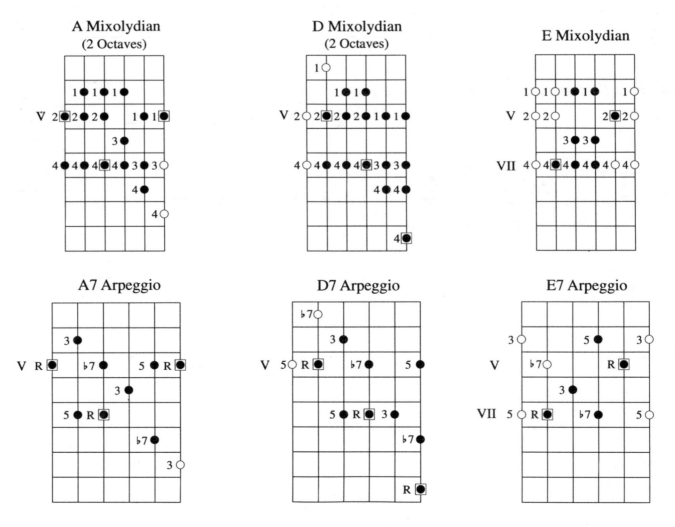

You should keep in mind that the forms in figure H are moveable patterns. The pattern for the D Mixolydian, for example (root on the 5th string, 5th fret), can be used to play an E Mixolydian mode by playing the entire pattern 2 frets higher (root on the 5th string, 7th fret).

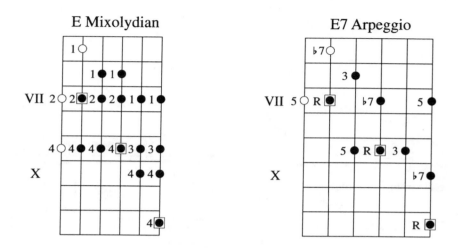

Ex. 34

Ex. 35

The "chord-scale" approach is useful when you want to match a mode to a specific chord type. The Scale - Chord relationships chart at the end of the book illustrates the different chord types that the modes can be matched with.

31

Probably one of the most interesting approaches to improvising is to mix the two soloing styles together (the Blues approach and the chord-scale approach). Example 36 shows the use of the Blues approach (scale based on a single root note) for part of the Blues progression, and the use of the chord-scale approach for other parts of the progression, for an approach to soloing that gives the soloist a great deal of flexibility.

Ex. 36

Combination Blues

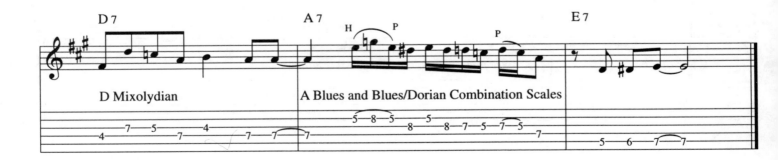

An interesting thing to note is that "individual" blues scales can be used for "each" chord in the Blues progression in the same way Mixolydian modes were matched to each chord. For example, you could use an E blues scale for the E7 chord, and a D blues scale for the D7 chord along with the A blues scale for the A7 chord. Since the A blues and A Mixolydian scales were interchangeable for the A7 chord, you can use this idea for the other chords.

In both soloing approaches that we've just studied (the blues approach and the chord-scale approach), we have applied the modes in a new way as compared to how the modes were first introduced. Since we needed Mixolydian modes built on different root notes, we used Mixolydian shapes starting on different root notes. You can find the "parent" or original key a mode is derived from by backtracking to the I chord from a modes numbered position in a key (ii or V, etc.). For example, for an A Mixolydian mode (because the Mixolydian is built on the fifth degree of a major scale) we think of the note "A" as the fifth degree in the key of "D" major. For the A Dorian mode you would think of the Dorian as being built on the "2nd" degree of a major scale, therefore "A" is the 2nd degree of G major. Figure I shows the original or parent keys for the modes that were used in both soloing approaches in the Blues chord progression.

Figure I

A Dorian	-	built on the 2nd degree of	G major
A Mixolydian	-	" " " 5th " "	D major
D Mixolydian	-	" " " 5th " "	G major
E Mixolydian	-	" " " 5th " "	A major

While it is helpful at times to know the parent key that a mode is derived from, it is also very important to memorize the "shapes" of the different modes because of the many times you will need to start modes off of different root notes. The mode shapes that are initially the most important to memorize (because of their frequent use in contemporary soloing), are the Ionian (or major scale), the Dorian, the Mixolydian and the Aeolian (or natural minor scale). You can refer to the Mode - Arpeggio guide at the end of this book to give you shapes in different positions.

Mixing Pentatonics – Mixing Elements

By combining elements, such as modes with pentatonic scales, we can have greater flexibility melodically. We can pair the A Dorian mode and the A minor pentatonic scale together because the A Dorian mode contains all of the notes in the A minor pentatonic. We can pair the A Mixolydian mode with the A major pentatonic scale because the A Mixolydian mode contains all of the notes in the A major pentatonic (ex. 37).

● = Root   ○ = Additional notes in position above or below the root notes.

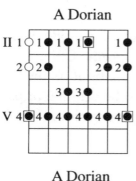

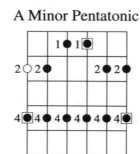

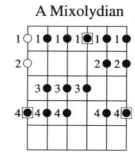

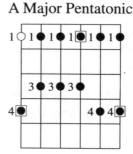

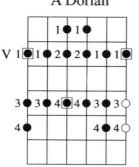

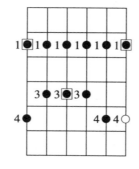

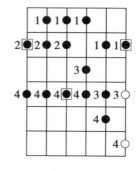

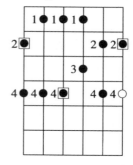

Fingers 2 & 3 can be used on the third string in place of fingers 3 & 4 to accomodate different note patterns.

Fingers 1 & 3 can be used on the first and second strings in place of fingers 2 & 4 for different note patterns. In addition, the 2nd finger can be used on the third string in place of the 3rd finger.

Ex. 37

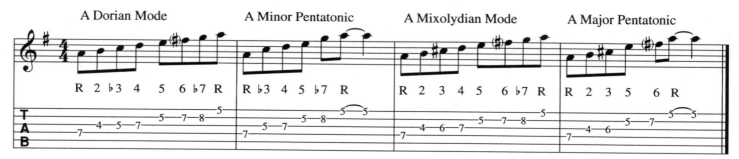

Example 38 uses the A Dorian mode along with the A minor pentatonic scale.

Ex. 38

34

Example 39 uses the A Dorian / A minor pentatonic combination for the first two measures, but uses the A Mixolydian / A major pentatonic combination over the A7 chord because the Mixolydian mode contains all of the notes in the A7 chord. By mixing elements you create a contrast melodically.

Ex. 39

Example 40 uses a 12 bar Blues progression to illustrate mixing modes and scales further.

Ex. 40

35

Shifting Key Centers

Because most Jazz tunes don't stay in the same key throughout the entire song, we need to explore a way of adapting to the shifting of key centers temporarily. In the key of G for example, if we have the progression Bm7 - Em7 - Am7 - D7 to Gmaj7, this progression adheres to the diatonic (staying within the key) iii - vi - ii -V - I pattern (ex. 41). But if there was an E7 instead of an Em7, then we can't use the basic diatonic approach for improvising (ex. 42).

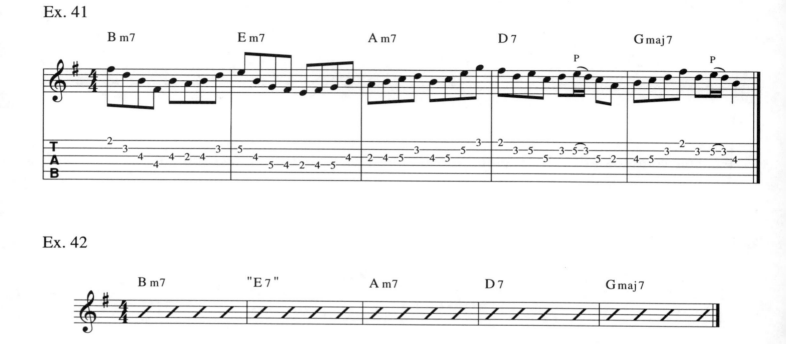

Ex. 41

Ex. 42

In Jazz you will find many minor 7 to dominant 7 chord changes that don't fit the original key. In these cases, you can think of these chord changes as being ii and V chords from a temporary key. It's easy to determine what that temporary key is (or essentially the original key that the chords came from) by counting backwards one whole step from the root of the minor 7 or "ii" chord. For example, with a Bm7 chord the root is one whole step above A, so Bm7 would be the ii chord in the key of A major (built on the second degree). E7 would then be the V chord in A major, a fifth away from the root A (built on the fifth degree). So using the A major scale (or A major as the temporary key), you would get a B Dorian mode (and Bm7 arpeggio) to go with the Bm7 chord and an E Mixolydian mode (and E7 arpeggio) to go with the E7 chord (ex. 43).

In example 44 we can incorporate this concept for the Bm7 and E7 chords, then use the key of G major for the Am7, D7, and Gmaj7 chords which are the ii, V, and I chords in the key of G. A good routine for practice, is to improvise over a repeated Bm7 - Em7 - Am7 - D7 chord pattern (iii - vi - ii - V from example 41) to get used to staying within a key. Then improvise over a repeated Bm7 - E7 - Am7 - D7 chord pattern (ii / A ,V / A, ii / G,V / G from example 44) to get used to shifting key centers.

Ex. 43

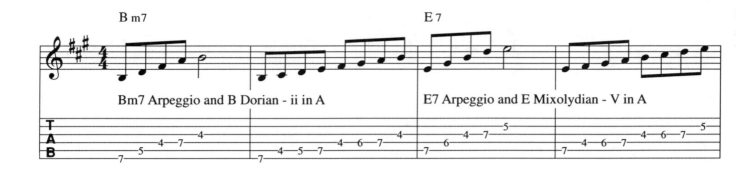

We will look at this approach in another key, using the key of C Major. In the key of C the diatonic iii - vi - ii - V - I pattern would be the chords Em7, Am7, Dm7, G7 to Cmaj7. But, if there was an A7 instead of the Am7, then we would see a minor 7 to dominant 7 relationship between the Em7 and A7. In this case we would use the key of D major temporarily (Em7 being the ii and A7 being the V chord in D major) to improvise over the Em7 to A7. Then we would return to the key of C to improvise over the Dm7, G7, and Cmaj7 chords (ex. 45). This approach can be applied to any key, and should be thought of when you see successive minor 7 to dominant 7 chord patterns.

Ex. 45

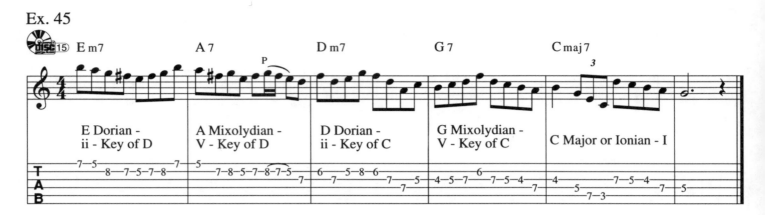

Example 46 uses minor to dominant chord combinations in a Blues progression.

Ex. 46

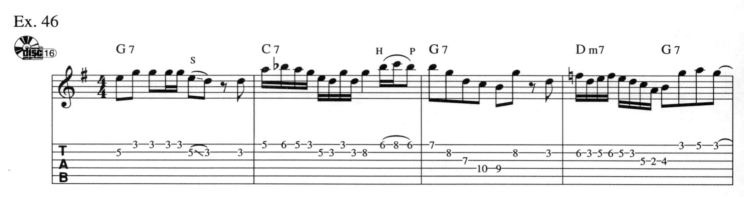

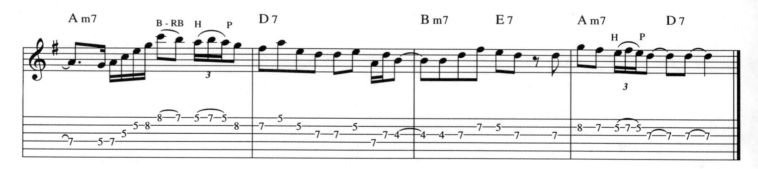

Example 47 shows another group of chords that can be used as the "turnaround" in bars 11 and 12 of the 12 bar Blues progression in example 46.

Ex. 47

Introducing Chromaticism

Many people, when confronted with the idea of chromaticism, are confused because there are 12 tones (half steps) to choose from. Aside from the most obvious use, which would be to play the 12 tones in order as a scale, we need to explore a way to incorporate chromatic notes into soloing.

In order to understand how to use chromaticism, let's look back at our original elements, the scale and arpeggio. When the arpeggio notes are thought of as reinforcing tones, then the scale can work around these tones effectively. Chromatic notes can also be played around the arpeggio notes in a similar way, to enhance the reinforcing characteristics of the arpeggio tones. If you think of "aiming" towards the chord tones (arpeggio notes), the chromatic notes can function as passing tones in between or around the chord tones to create tension until arriving at the chord tone.

One common use, is to approach the chord tones (1, 3, 5, 7) from above or below with successive half steps. The use of 3, 4, or 5 half steps can be very effective and they can be used in different combinations. Successive half-steps can be particularly effective when joining chord tones (for example the note B going up chromatically to D in a G major arpeggio) and also when interweaved with scale notes and arpeggios (ex. 48).

Ex. 48

Another way to incorporate chromaticism is to approach the chord tones from a diatonic step (scale step) above, and from a half step below (ex. 49).

Ex. 49

In examples 50 and 51 you can observe the use of chromaticism to join scale notes and to enhance arpeggio notes.

Ex. 50

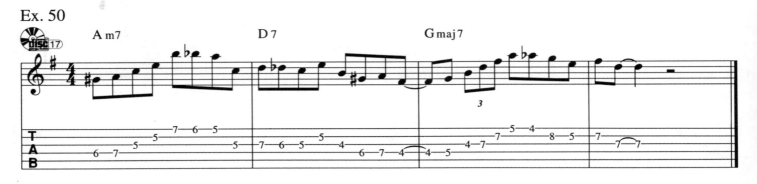

Ex. 51

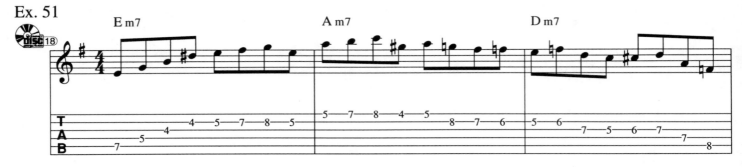

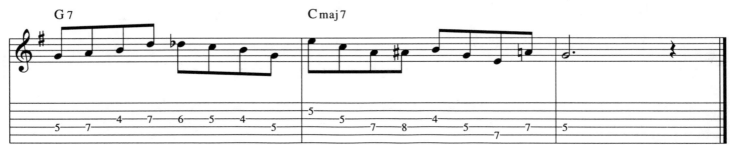

Aiming and Joining Techniques For Chromaticism

When using chromaticism it is helpful to think of arpeggio tones or even pentatonic scale tones as resting points. Figures J and K show neighboring tones a half step below arpeggio and pentatonic scale tones which are "aimed" toward as points of resolution. This creates a sense of tension and release. It sounds more interesting when these shapes are not played in strict order, but rather in combinations with other scale and arpeggio sequences (ex. 52 and 53). In Figure L you can see shapes created by "joining" or linking notes in the pentatonic scale. These shapes also sound best when not played in strict order as shown in examples 54 and 55.

Figure J

● = Root   ○ = Chromatic 1/2 step neighboring tones
Numbers refer to the interval from the root

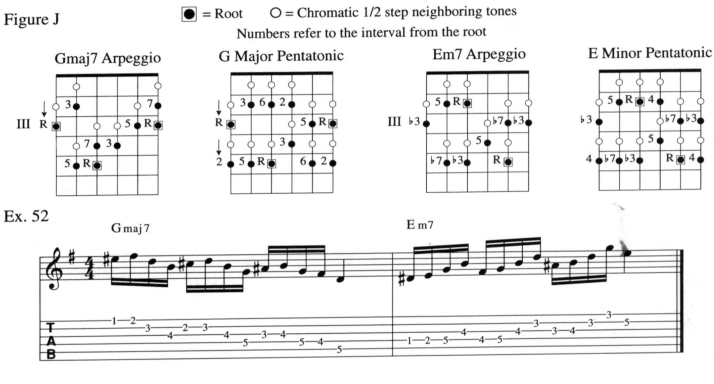

Ex. 52

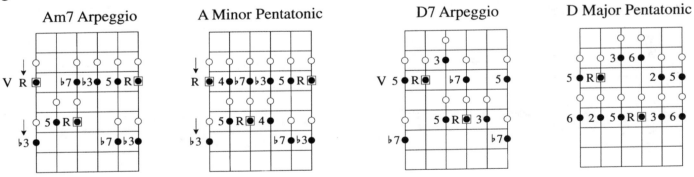

Figure K

Ex. 53

41

Figure L

O = Chromatic joining tones.

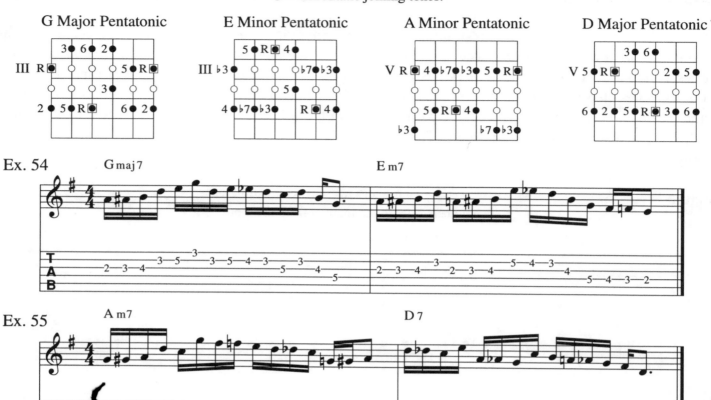

G Major Pentatonic   E Minor Pentatonic   A Minor Pentatonic   D Major Pentatonic

Ex. 54

Ex. 55

By combining the ideas of "aiming" and "joining" with scale notes and arpeggios, interesting and unique melodic lines can be created (ex. 56).

Ex. 56

Adding Chromatic Notes To Scales

You may notice that the Blues scale is created by adding a chromatic "joining" tone to the A minor pentatonic scale. By adding a chromatic joining tone to the A major pentatonic we can create a hybrid scale. This scale called the major pentatonic hybrid, will work with the A Mixolydian mode just as the A major pentatonic did (ex. 57).

○ = Added chromatic note

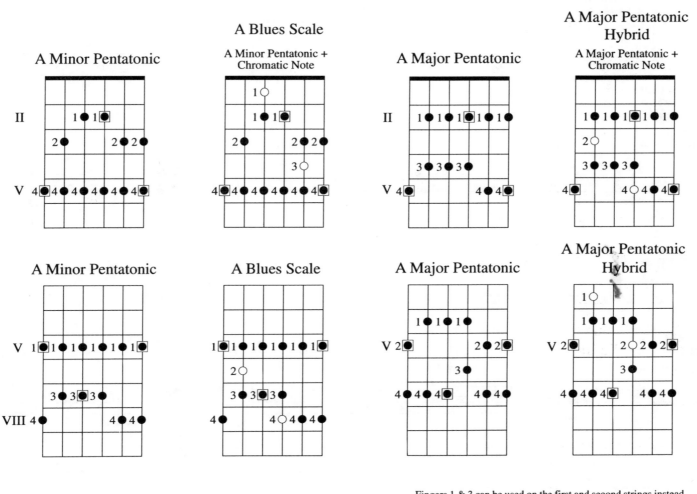

Fingers 1 & 3 can be used on the first and second strings instead of fingers 2 & 4 as an alternate fingering

Ex. 57

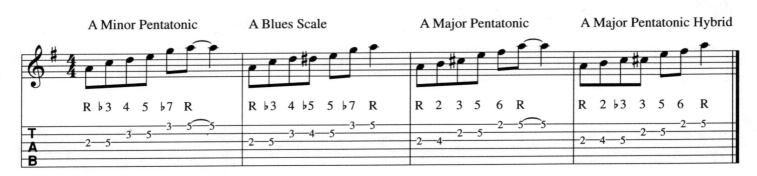

By adding a chromatic half-step between the seventh degree (♭7 interval) and root of the Mixolydian mode, we create a scale that is referred to as the Be-Bop Dominant scale (ex. 58 and 59).

Ex. 58 - A Mixolydian Chromatic or Be-Bop Dominant Scale

The 1st and 2nd fingers can be used for the notes on the first string as an alternate fingering.

Ex. 59   A 7

Example 60 shows how combining elements expands the overall melodic character.

Ex. 60

Chord Extensions And Extended Arpeggios

The term extensions or extended tones refers to 9th, 11th and 13th intervals above the root of a seventh chord or arpeggio. In an extended arpeggio the extensions (9, 11, 13) can be thought of as a three note arpeggio built above a seventh arpeggio (R, 3, 5, 7). A simple way to approach playing the diatonic arpeggios (or chord tones) extended through the 13th, is to play every other note in each of the modes built on the different degrees of the major scale. For example, play the first note of a mode and skip the second note, then play the third note of the mode and skip the fourth note and so on, until you have played seven different notes for each mode. This pattern will produce the proper sequence of intervals needed to give you extended arpeggios for each degree of the major scale.

Example 61 illustrates the diatonic arpeggios extended through the 13th in the key of G major. The iii (B minor) extended arpeggio has a ♭13 interval which may sound dissonant when played against the iii chord (Bm7). To alleviate this problem, when the arpeggio is played in order that ♭13 (G) can be resolved to a 5th (F♯) to create a sound of resolution. Similarly, in the vi (E minor) extended arpeggio the ♭13 interval creates the same problem when played against the vi (Em7) chord. This note can also be resolved to the 5th.

Diagrams for the Diatonic Arpeggios Extended through the 13th in the Key of G Major

Numbers refer to the interval from the root.

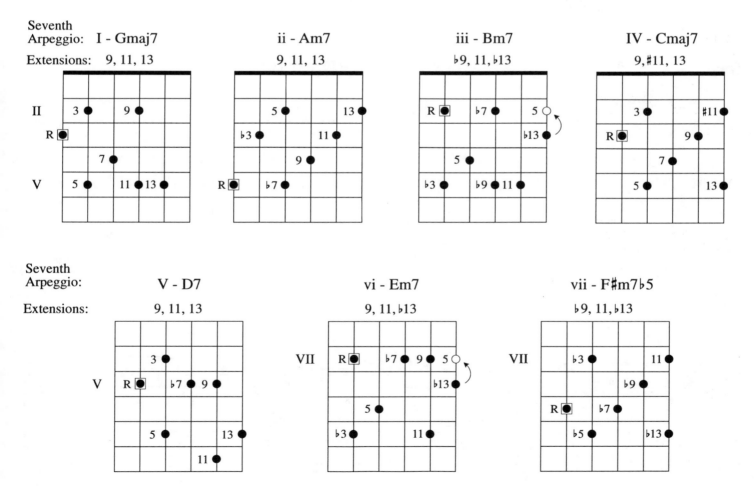

45

Ex. 61 - Extended Arpeggios in the Key of G Major

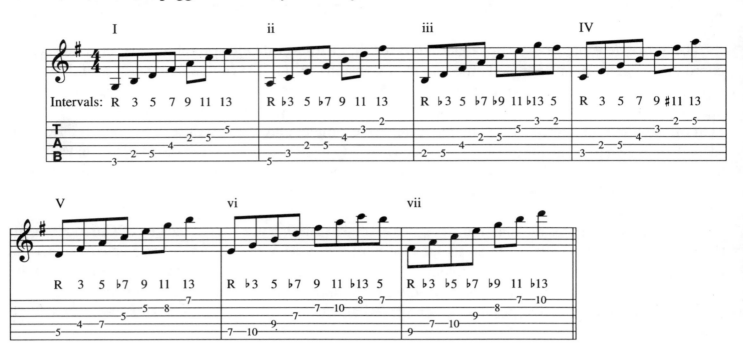

When you have temporary key situations you would use the extensions that pertain to the parent key or original key that the chords were built from. In example 62 you can see successive ii - V chord changes. The extended arpeggio for the Am7 and D7 chords would be derived from the key of G major (they are the ii and V chords from the key of G major). The Gm7 and C7 chords are the ii and V chords in the key of F major so consequently you would use the extensions derived from the key of F major.

Numbers refer to the interval from the root

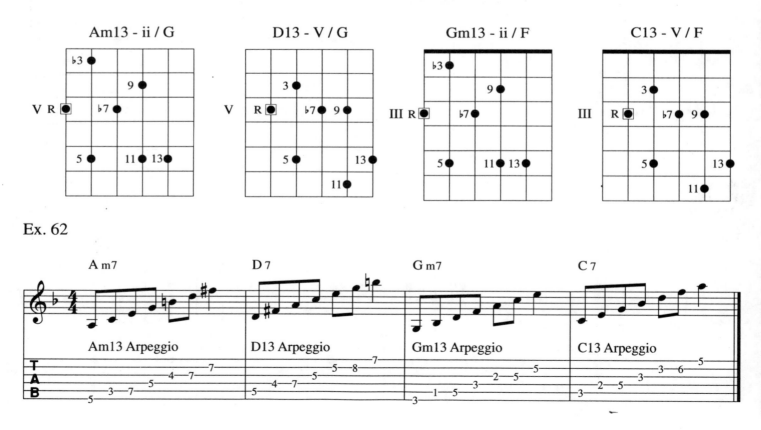

Ex. 62

46

One of the many interesting uses of the extended arpeggio is to accentuate different parts of the arpeggio. For example, the A minor extended arpeggio (based on the Dorian mode - extended through the 13th) has an Am7 arpeggio, a Cmaj7 arpeggio, an Em7 arpeggio, and a Gmaj7 arpeggio all contained within it (ex. 63). The A minor extended arpeggio tones can be used to improvise over Am7, Am6, Am9 and Am11 chords (ex. 64 and 65).

Ex. 63

Ex. 64

Ex. 65

Something to remember is that the extended arpeggios don't have to be played in order, and the extensions (9, 11, 13) can be mixed with the lower part of the arpeggio (1, 3, 5, 7) in the same register for some interesting sounds (ex. 66).

Ex. 66

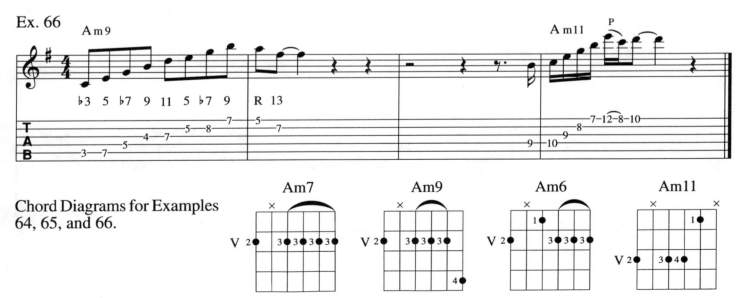

Chord Diagrams for Examples 64, 65, and 66.

47

Chromaticism can be used around the extended arpeggios in the same way that we saw introduced earlier with the seventh arpeggios. The extended arpeggio tones can be approached chromatically with 3, 4, or 5 half steps and you get the same kind of effect that we did before. You can also approach these extended chord tones from a diatonic step above and a half step below as shown in example 67. The melodic pattern in example 67 is referred to as "melodic sequencing"

Ex. 67

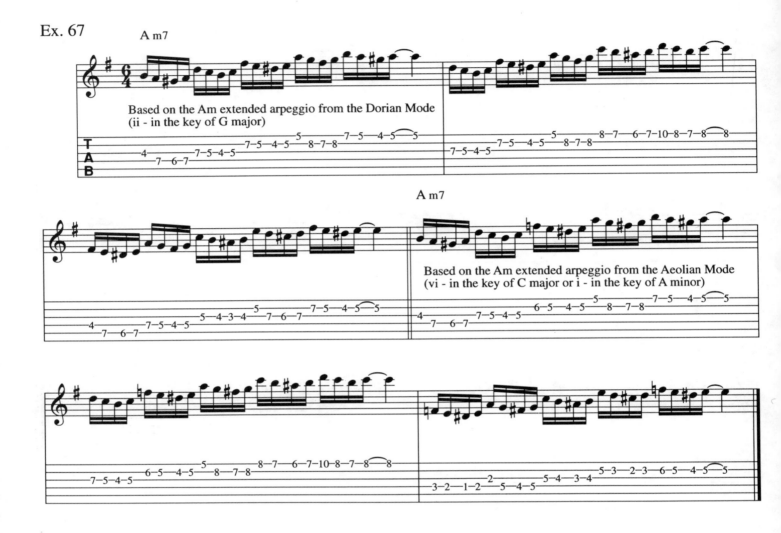

Examples 68 through 72 show some melodic ideas that combine extended arpeggios with scales and chromaticism. These examples give you an idea of how all of the elements - scales, arpeggios, and chromaticism, work together to make a musical statement.

Ex. 68

48

Ex. 69

Ex. 70

Ex. 71

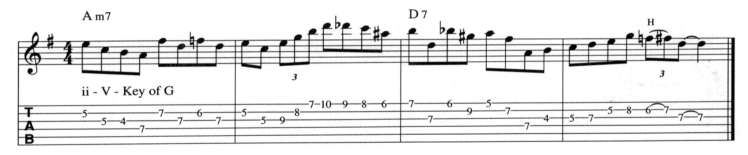

Ex. 72

Minor Keys

The natural minor scale is the primary (or parent) scale in a minor key in the same way that the major scale is the primary scale in a major key. Before we learn how this scale relates to a minor key center, let's first look at how the minor scale relates to the major scale. Each major scale has a relative minor scale that is built off of the sixth degree. These are called relative scales because the notes used in both scales are the same (ex. 73). The difference with a minor key is that the key centers around the root of the minor scale as the "tonic" or 1st degree.

Ex. 73

A Natural Minor Scale Fingerings.

● = Root   O = Additional scale notes in position above or below the root notes.

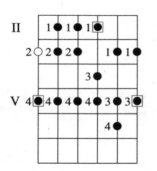 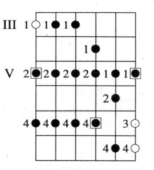  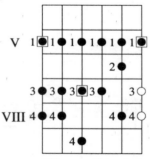

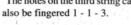
The notes on the third string can also be fingered 1 - 1 - 3.

(Alternate Fingering)

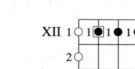 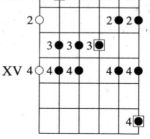  

Essentially all of the chords built off of an A minor scale are the same as C major, but now we have a different starting point (fig. M). You will notice with the key of A minor, that the V chord has a minor quality. Through the use of borrowing from the harmonic minor scale, we can change this to a dominant quality (which is the typical quality for V chords). But for now we will use the v minor chord because some interesting chord progressions can be derived (ex. 75).

Figure M - C Major and A Minor Chords Compared

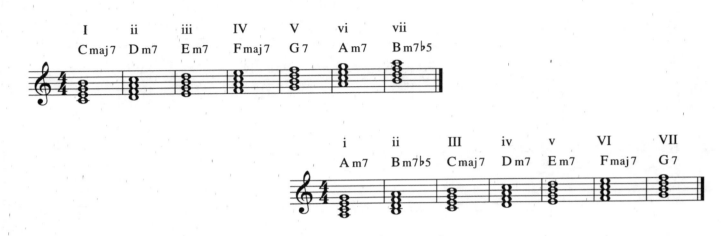

The roman numerals for the seventh chords built on the seventh scale degree in major (vii) and the second scale degree in minor (ii) may sometimes be followed by the symbol "ø", however the abbreviations are used throughout this book.

Ex. 74 - Chords Built in the Key of A Minor Voiced for the Guitar

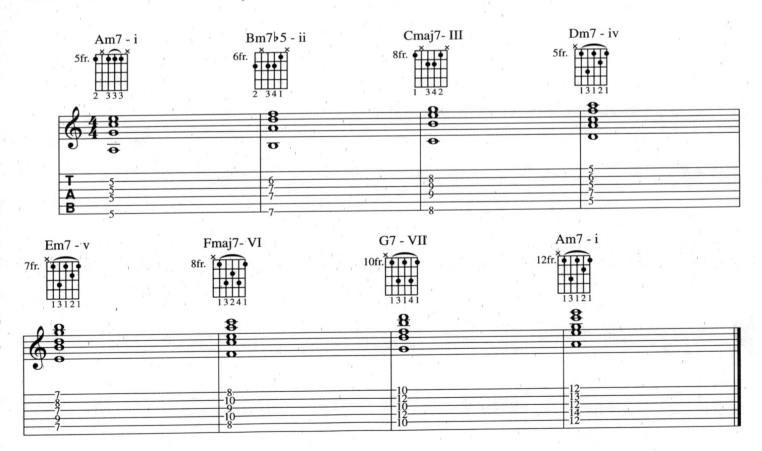

51

Ex. 75

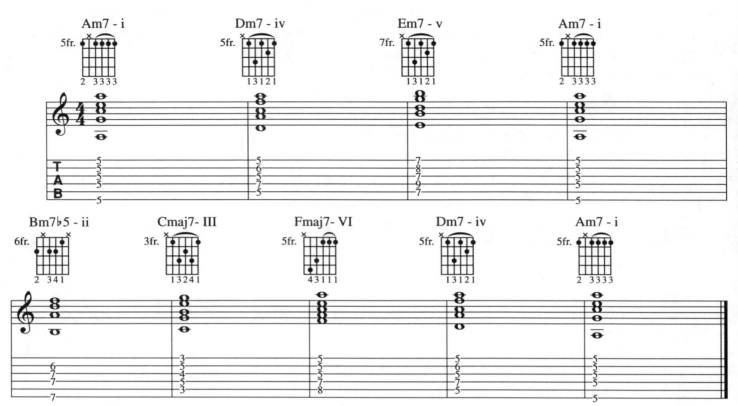

Because the chords for the keys of A minor and C major relate, the modes will transfer as well. Though the "numbering" will change, the names and order of modes will not. In other words, even though we start with the Aeolian mode for a minor key (which is now i), the modes appear in the same order as they do in a major key and will be paired with the same chord type (fig. N). Example 76 pairs the arpeggios (broken chords) with the modes (chord scales) for the key of A minor.

Figure N

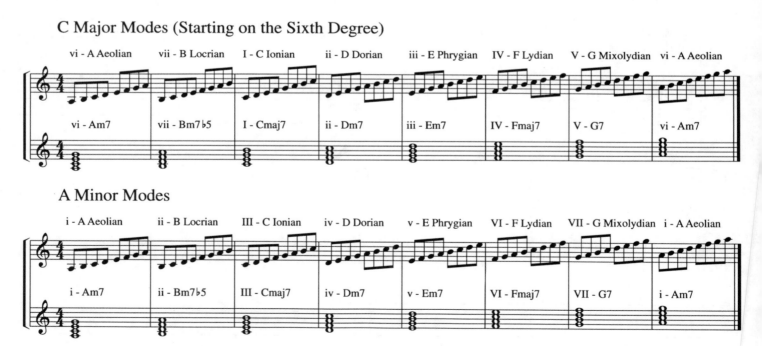

Diagrams for example 76 – A natural minor modes and arpeggios

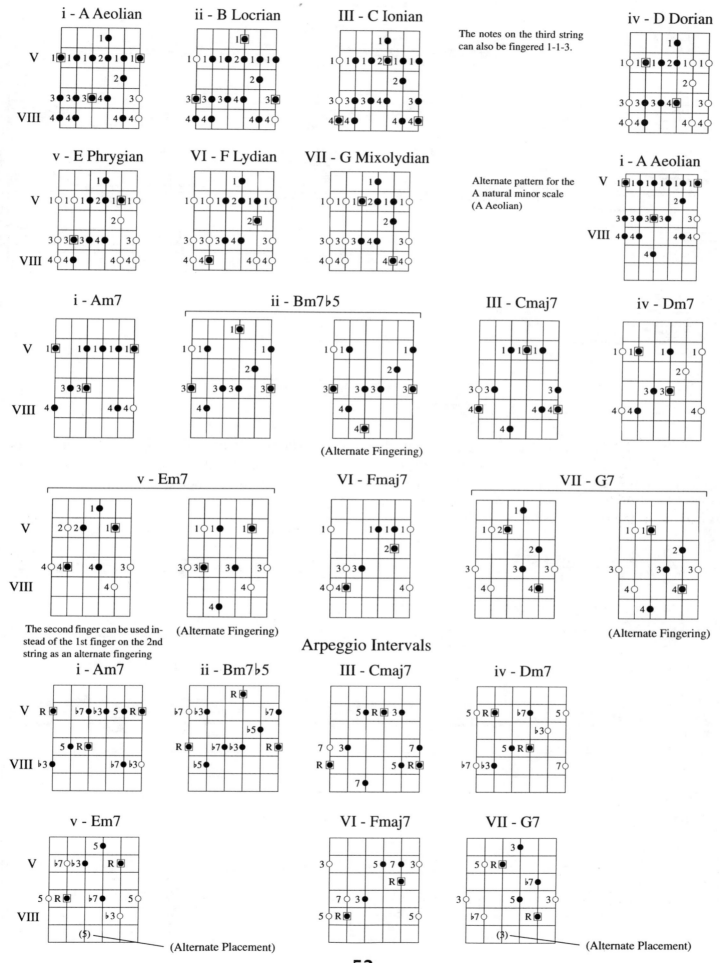

The notes on the third string can also be fingered 1-1-3.

Alternate pattern for the A natural minor scale (A Aeolian)

(Alternate Fingering)

(Alternate Fingering)

The second finger can be used instead of the 1st finger on the 2nd string as an alternate fingering

(Alternate Fingering)

(Alternate Fingering)

Arpeggio Intervals

(Alternate Placement)

(Alternate Placement)

Ex. 76

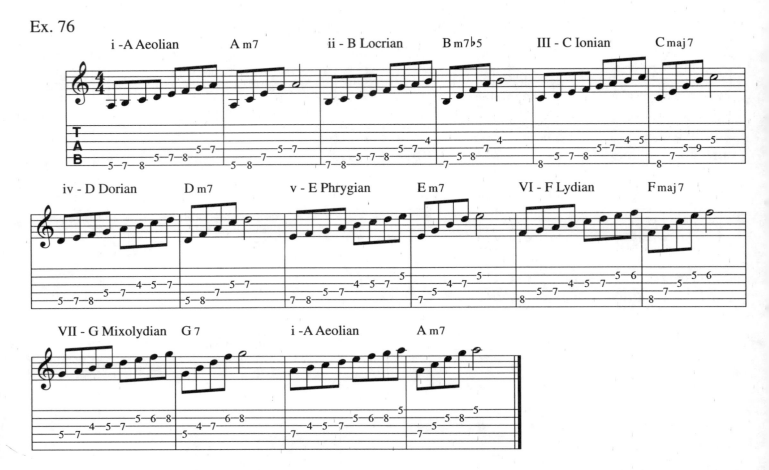

In addition to the modes and arpeggios based on the natural minor scale, the blues scale can be used for improvising in a minor key. Example 77 is based on a 12 bar minor Blues progression (with a minor v chord) and uses scales and arpeggios from the key of A minor with the A blues scale.

Ex. 77

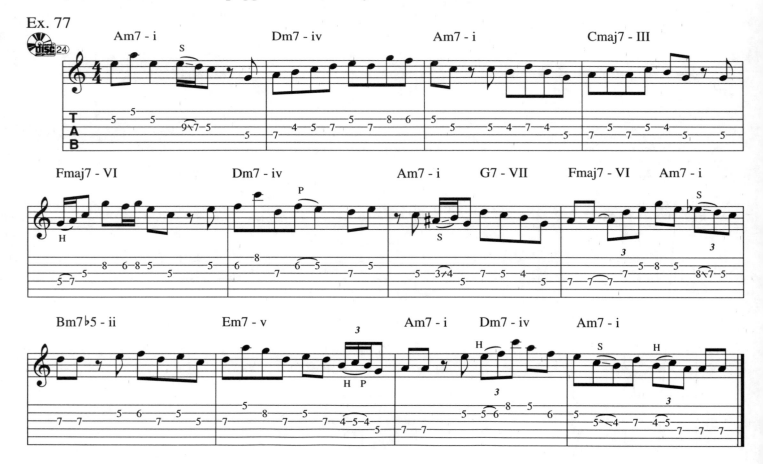

The Harmonic Minor Scale

The harmonic minor scale is essentially a natural minor scale with a raised 7th degree (creating a leading tone to the root of the tonic or I chord - ex. 78).

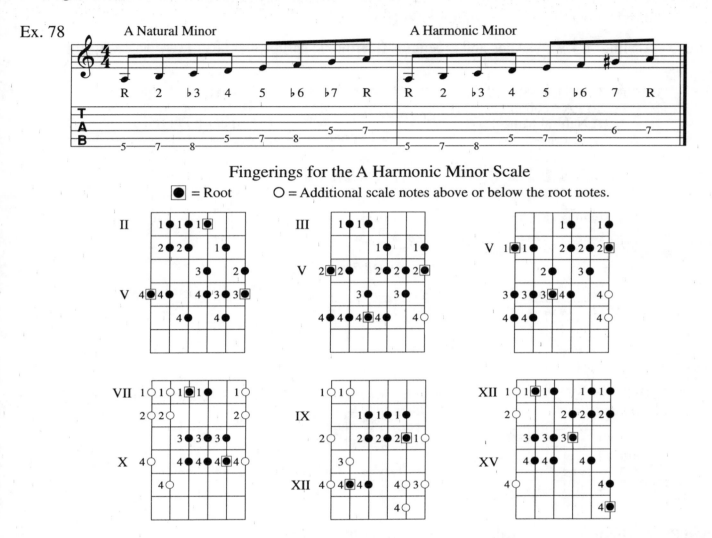

Ex. 78

A Natural Minor   A Harmonic Minor

R   2   ♭3   4   5   ♭6   ♭7   R   R   2   ♭3   4   5   ♭6   7   R

Fingerings for the A Harmonic Minor Scale

● = Root   O = Additional scale notes above or below the root notes.

The harmonic minor scale can be used to facilitate the change of the minor V chord to a dominant quality by raising the "third" of the V chord 1/2 step. The technique of altering the third of the dominant chord in this way is called "borrowing" from the harmonic minor scale. In this way the other chords harmonized from the A natural minor scale retain the note G natural (♭7), only the V chord is changed (ex. 79).

Ex. 79

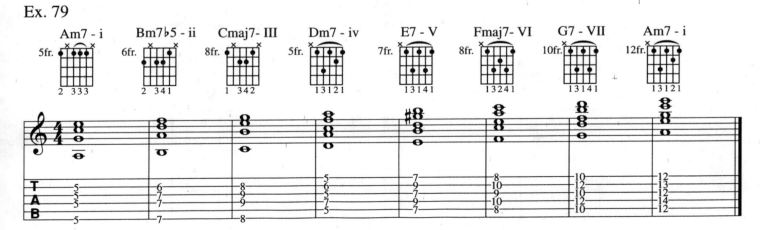

Am7 - i   Bm7♭5 - ii   Cmaj7- III   Dm7 - iv   E7 - V   Fmaj7- VI   G7 - VII   Am7 - i

55

Figure O illustrates scale and arpeggio patterns for the i, ii, and V chords in the key of A minor with the V chord using the G♯ from the A harmonic minor scale for its scale and arpeggio (the E altered Phrygian scale is essentially built off of the 5th degree of the A harmonic minor scale). An important area of the fingerboard used for the minor key ii - V - i progression is where the root of the tonic (i) chord is on the 5th string. While this may be high on the fretboard for this particular key (12th position), you will find these shapes useful when playing in other minor keys (fig. P).

Figure O - A Minor ii - V - i scales and arpeggios (Harmonic Minor scale form for the V Chord)

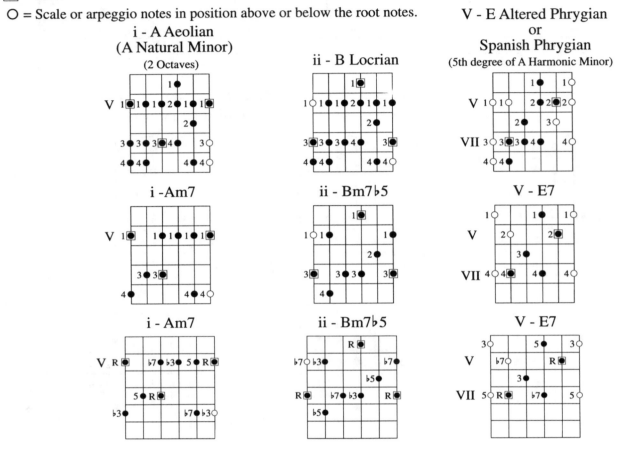

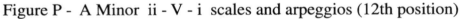

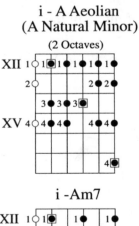

Figure P - A Minor ii - V - i scales and arpeggios (12th position)

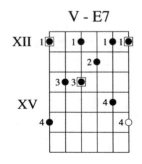

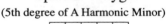

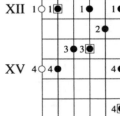

Figure P - Cont.

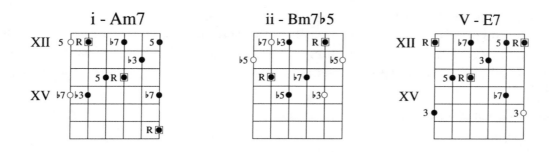

Examples 80 and 81 show ii - V - i minor chord progressions using a dominant quality V chord. In example 81 note how the A harmonic minor scale is used to create chromatic neighboring tones when playing over the Bm7♭5 and Am chords.

Ex. 80

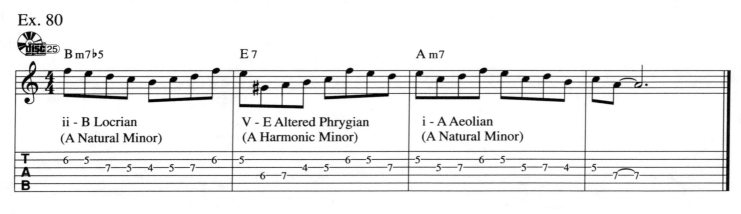

Ex. 81

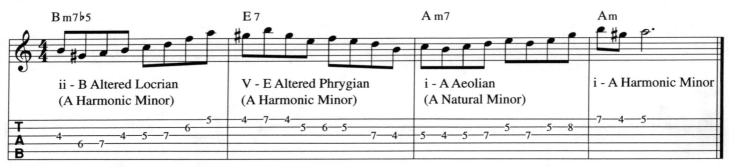

Notice in the second measure of both examples 80 and 81 the note F natural which is a ♭9th interval from the root of the E dominant 7 chord. Since this interval falls naturally within the altered Phrygian scale, it means this scale can be used over a dominant 7♭9 chord (referred to as an altered dominant).

If the V chord in examples 80 and 81 had a ♯9 (E7♯9), a problem would arise because the E altered Phrygian scale (5th degree of A harmonic minor) has a G♯ to cover the third of the chord but doesn't address the ♯9 (F double sharp). On the other hand the E Phrygian scale (5th degree of A natural minor) can cover the ♯9 (G natural is enharmonic to F double sharp), but it doesn't cover the third of the dominant chord (G♯). It is necessary therefore to create a scale (or scales) which would use elements of both Phrygian scales to be able to address both the 3rd and the ♯9 of a dominant 7♯9 chord. One possibility is to combine the notes from both the E Phrygian and the E altered Phrygian scales (5th degree of A natural minor and A harmonic minor) to get an E combination Phrygian scale which will work with Dominant 7♯9 and Dominant 7♭9 chords.

Another possibility is to use the E altered Phrygian scale notes (5th degree of A harmonic minor) for the first octave, and then use the E Phrygian scale notes (5th degree of A natural minor) for the second octave to get an E "hybrid" Phrygian scale. The "different" second octave will cover either the ♭9 or ♯9 of an E altered dominant chord, while the third of the chord (G♯) is taken care of in the first octave (ex. 82). The combination Phrygian and hybrid Phrygian scales will also work with dominant 7♯5, dominant 7♯5♯9 and dominant 7♯5♭9 chords because the ♯5 is enharmonic (same pitch) to a ♭6 interval which occurs in both of these scales.

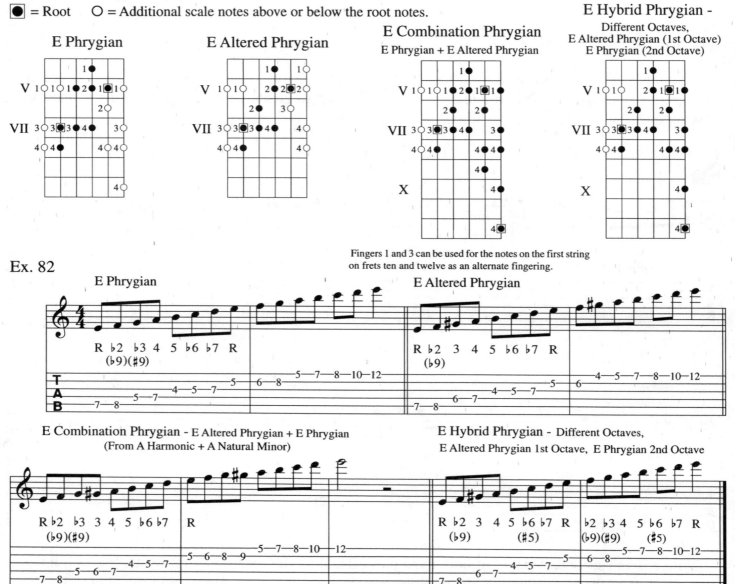

Ex. 82

Fingers 1 and 3 can be used for the notes on the first string on frets ten and twelve as an alternate fingering.

Example 83 shows the effect of using the hybrid Phrygian scale over an altered dominant chord in a ii - V - i minor chord progression.

Ex. 83

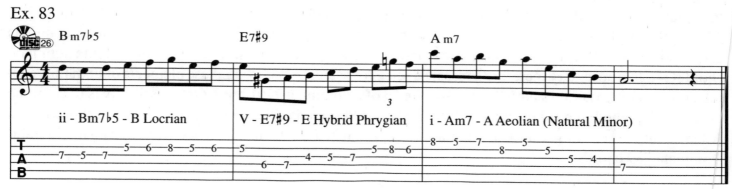

More About Extensions

Arpeggios can be extended through the 13th in a minor key using the natural minor scale in the same way as was done before in the major key (using the major scale). By playing every other note in each of the modes built on the different degrees of the minor scale, we can derive arpeggios through the 13th. The only difference will be for the V chord in a minor key where the third is altered by borrowing from the harmonic form of the minor scale (note that the ♭9 interval naturally occurs in this scale - ex. 84). Notice that in the case of the i and the V chords, the ♭13 interval can be resolved to the 5th for a smoother sound. You will run into altered dominant chords that have a raised 5th in which case the ♭13 is enharmonic and can be left alone.

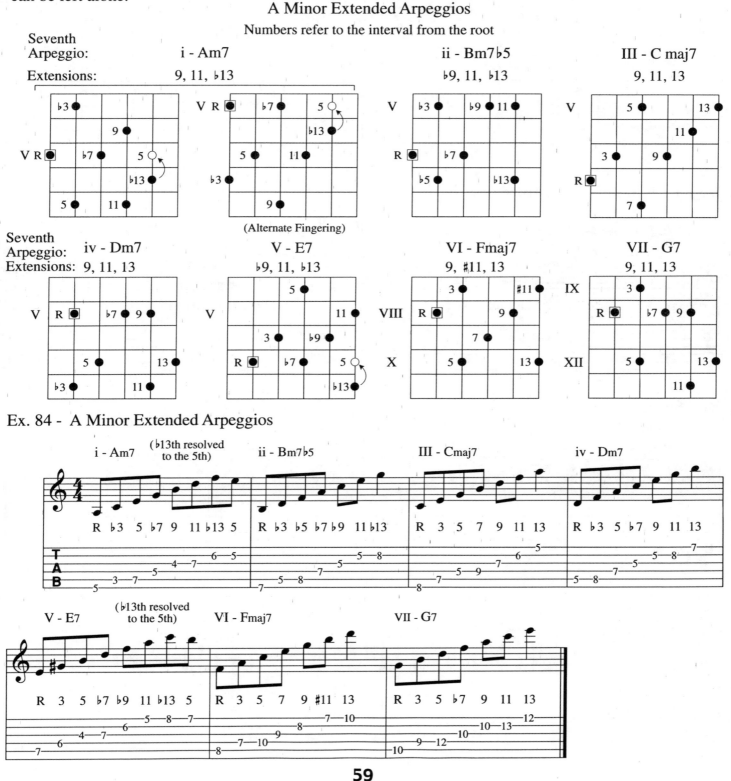

Ex. 84 - A Minor Extended Arpeggios

59

An interesting arpeggio can be built for the V chord from the E hybrid Phrygian scale, by using both the ♭9 and ♯9 intervals (resolving the ♭13th to the 5th). The hybrid Phrygian scale can also be used to create an interesting arpeggio which could be used over a dom. 7♯5♯9 chord by leaving the ♭13th unresolved (to create an enharmonic ♯5 - ex. 85). As we saw before with the major extensions, the extensions here can be very effective when played out of sequence and when mixed with the lower part of the arpeggio in the same register (ex. 86).

Hybrid Derived Extended Arpeggios

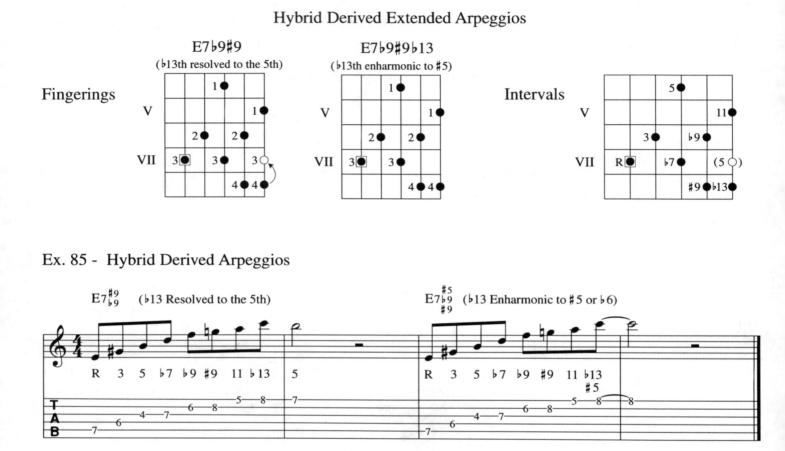

Ex. 85 - Hybrid Derived Arpeggios

Ex. 86

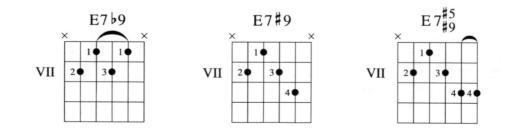

Minor Blues

Now that we have explored some soloing elements for dominant and altered dominant V chords found in a minor key, we can tackle a minor blues progression with a dominant quality V chord. The A natural minor and A blues scales can be used for the progression in example 87 with the E altered Phrygian scale used for dominant 7 and dominant 7♭9 V chords (E7 and E7♭9) and E combination Phrygian and E hybrid Phrygian scales used for dominant 7, dominant 7♭9 and dominant 7#9 chords (E7, E7♭9, E7#9).

Ex. 87

Minor Alteration

Chromatic notes can be used to enhance arpeggio notes and scales in a minor key in the same way as we saw before for a major key. The same devices can be used such as approaching chord tones with successive half steps (from above or below) or approaching chord tones from a scale step above and from a half step below. Approaching the chord tones from a scale step above and from a half step below is especially interesting with the E7 chord when using the E altered Phrygian scale (5th degree of A harmonic minor) because this sequence creates half steps above and below the root, 3rd, and 5th of the chord (ex. 88).

Ex. 88

In example 89 notice that we have the same chord progression as we did in example 87 but in the written solo chromatic notes have been added with the scale and arpeggio notes.

Ex. 89

Chromatic Blues

Superimposing

Superimposing involves using different musical elements over a chord to create special sounds or colors. These elements may come from the key center a chord is related to or may be borrowed from another source. There are two distinct types of superimposing, scalar which involves using modes or pentatonics, and chordal which involves using triads (3 note arpeggios) and 7th arpeggios (4 notes).

When Superimposing triads or seventh arpeggios over a chord, you can essentially use all of the arpeggios that come from a harmonized scale (a scale which matches the chord type) "over" the chord being played. In the case of an Amaj7 chord (thought of as a I chord), you can use all of the triads or seventh arpeggios that are derived from an A major scale over the Amaj7 chord (ex. 90).

Diagrams for the A Major Diatonic 7th Arpeggios

Numbers Refer to Fingering - Arpeggios are Voiced (R, 3, 5, 7)

● = Root   O = Additional notes above the root note that don't make up a complete octave

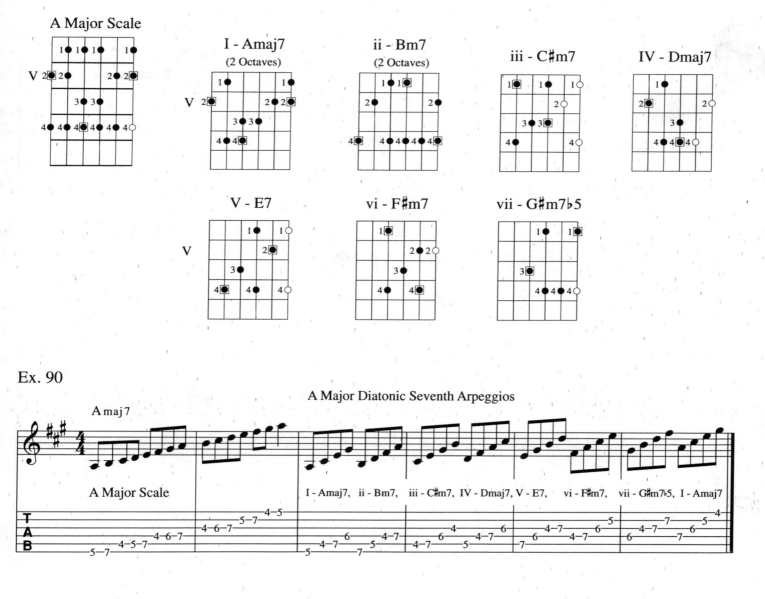

Ex. 90

A Major Diatonic Seventh Arpeggios

63

Seventh arpeggios and triads built off of the A major scale can be arranged so that they outline the notes of the A Major extended arpeggio (which is built off of the A major scale - examples 91, 92, and 93).

Ex. 91

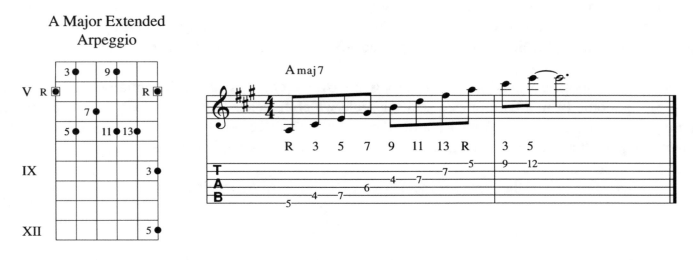

Ex. 92 - Four Note Arpeggios Outlining the A Major Extended Arpeggio

Ex. 93 - Triads Outlining the A Major Extended Arpeggio

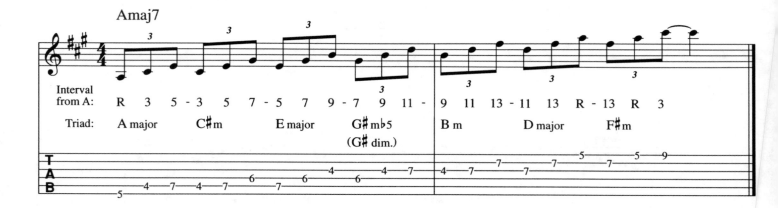

64

Example 94 shows the extensions (9, 11, 13) revoiced to a lower octave.

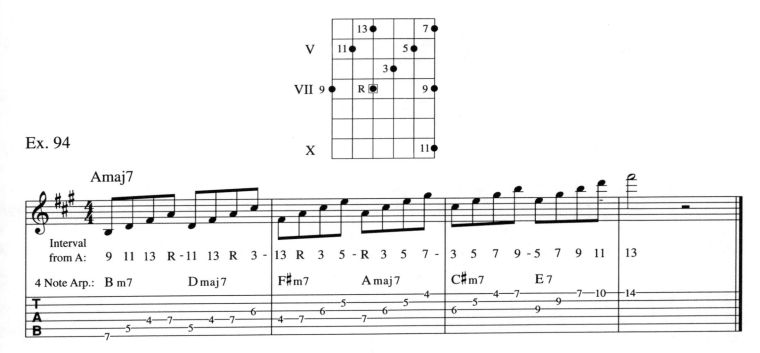

Ex. 94

This approach can be applied to any scale. By building triads or seventh arpeggios off of each degree of a mode, you can come up with interesting melodic ideas over the chord type associated with the mode.

Examples 95 through 98 illustrate how superimposing triads and four note arpeggios can work over different chord types.

Ex. 95 - Superimposing Using the A Major Scale

Ex. 96 - Superimposing Using the A Lydian Mode

Chord Diagram for Example 96

Ex. 97 - Superimposing Using the A Mixolydian Mode

Ex. 98 - Superimposing Using the A Dorian Mode

Superimposing Using Scales

The use of superimposing with scales refers to playing a scale or mode over a chord to create a particular sound. Superimposing allows you to use a scale derived from a source other than the key you are in, or to essentially use a scale that isn't "normally" matched with a chord type. This concept allows you to use a number of scales built on the same root and consequently produce many types of melodic coloration.

The first example of this would be the use of the Dorian mode in the Blues progression shown earlier. While the Dorian mode is normally played over a minor 7 chord, not a dominant 7 chord (the Mixolydian is normally used for that), the Dorian mode can be used because of its similarity to the blues scale and for the tonal coloration produced when played against the dominant 7 chord. Because of its use in Jazz, Blues, and Rock styles the Dorian mode is one of the more recognizable modes.

A very exotic sounding scale that can be played over a dominant 7 chord or even a basic (non-seventh) major chord is the altered Phrygian scale (built on the 5th degree of the harmonic minor scale). While this scale can be used over dominant chords with a flat 9th, it produces a special coloration when played over a regular dominant 7th chord (in place of the Mixolydian mode), or a major chord with no added 7th. This scale is popular in Rock soloing because it is easily applied over power chords. Because power chords are made up of only roots and fifths (no 3rds), this scale as well as the Dorian mode, the Mixolydian mode, and the Aeolian mode can be superimposed without any clashes.

Example 99 shows the use of the A hybrid Phrygian scale which is a combination of the A altered Phrygian and the A Phrygian scales (D harmonic minor and D natural minor parent scales). Example 100 shows the use of this scale in a chord progression. The A Hybrid Phrygian will work over the B♭ chord because there is a B♭ triad contained within the scale. For the C chord however, it is best to use the un-altered A Phrygian (D natural minor parent) to eliminate a clash with the note C♯ which is in the hybrid Phrygian form.

66

A Hybrid Phrygian

(A Altered Phrygian for two
octaves, A Phrygian thereafter)

A Phrygian

5th Degree of D Natural Minor
(Also 3rd Degree of F Major)

A Altered Phrygian

(5th Degree of D Harmonic Minor)

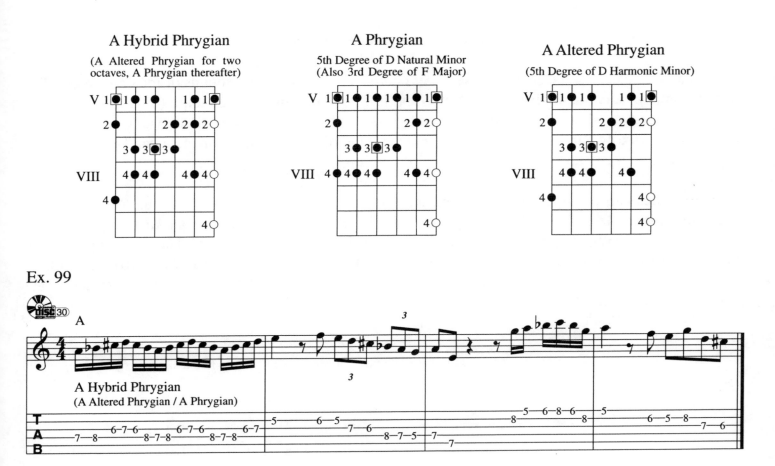

Ex. 99

A Hybrid Phrygian
(A Altered Phrygian / A Phrygian)

Ex.100

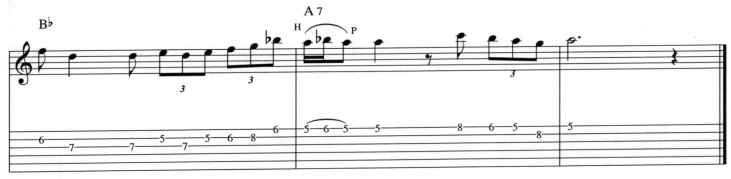

A Hybrid Phrygian

A Phrygian

Superimposing Using Pentatonics

Pentatonic scales can be superimposed over chords to create different sounds or melodic colors. The best example of a common use of superimposing is when an A minor pentatonic (or A blues scale) is played over an A dominant 7 chord in a Blues progression. Even though the ♭3rd interval (C natural) is not found in the Mixolydian mode which the dominant 7 chord is built from, this note can be used for the melodic tension it creates.

Pentatonics can be superimposed over chords to outline chord tones (R, 3rd, 5th, 7th) and chord extensions (9ths, 11ths, 13ths). For example, by using an E major pentatonic over an Amaj7 chord you are playing 5th, 6th (13th), maj7th, 2nd (9th), and 3rd intervals over the Amaj7 chord. The A major pentatonic outlines the root, and 2nd (9th), 3rd, 5th, and 6th (13th) intervals over the A chord (ex. 101). By mixing these two pentatonic scales together we can accentuate chord tones and chord extensions over an Amaj7 chord (ex. 102-103).

◉ = Root   ○ = Additional scale notes above or below the root notes.

E Major Pentatonic
Major Pentatonic a 5th Higher

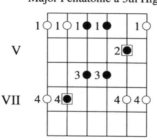

A Major Pentatonic
Major Pentatonic Based on the Chord Root

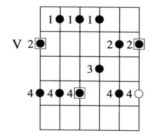

Fingers 1 & 3 can be used on the first and second strings in place of fingers 2 & 4 as an alternate fingering. In addition, the 2nd finger can be used on the third string in place of the third finger.

Ex. 101

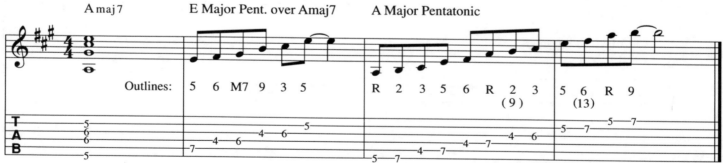

Ex. 102 - Combined Pentatonics

Ex. 103

By using the B major pentatonic over an Amaj7 chord, you play 2nd (9th), 3rd, ♯4th (♯11th), 6th (13th), and major 7th intervals over the Amaj7 chord. By combining the three pentatonics (A, B, and E major) you create the notes in the A Lydian mode (ex. 104). The "superimposing" of the Lydian mode (A Lydian = E major parent) over a tonic or I chord (Amaj7 - key of A major) is a popular device in Jazz and Fusion styles of music.

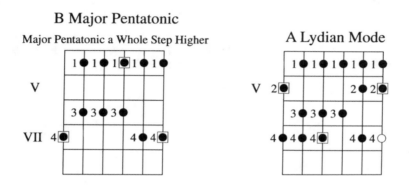

Ex. 104

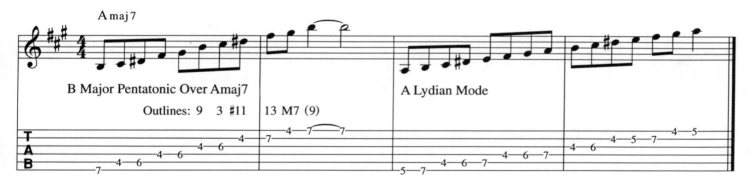

Ex. 105 - Combining the A Lydian Mode with the individual A, B, and E Pentatonics

Minor pentatonic scales can be superimposed over minor chords also. An E minor pentatonic scale can be superimposed over an Am7 chord to outline the root as well as 5th, ♭7th, 2nd (9th), and 4th (11th) intervals over the Am7 chord. Either the E minor pentatonic (minor pentatonic root a 5th higher than the chord root "A") or A minor pentatonic scales can be used with both the A Dorian mode and A natural minor scales (ex. 106). The B minor pentatonic can be superimposed over an Am7 chord to outline the root as well as 2nd (9th), 4th (11th), 5th, and 6th (13th) intervals over the Am7 chord. The B minor pentatonic can be used with the A Dorian mode, however, it is not used with the A natural minor scale (A Aeolian mode) because the 6th interval (above A) that the B minor pentatonic contains would clash with the ♭6 interval in the A natural minor scale. Example 107 shows that when the A minor pentatonic and B minor pentatonic scales are combined, they form the A Dorian mode.

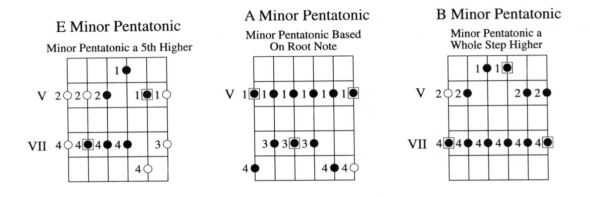

Ex. 106

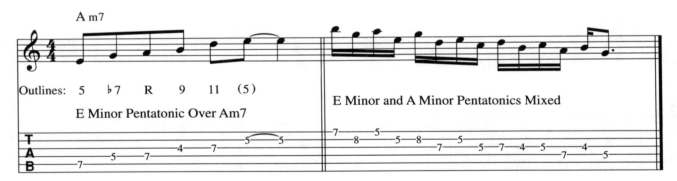

Ex. 107

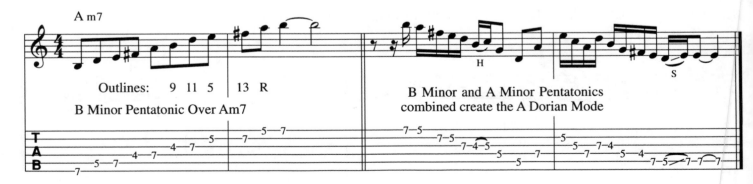

70

In the previous examples we have superimposed major pentatonics over a major chord and minor pentatonics over a minor chord. For the dominant 7th chord we will try a slightly different approach. The D major pentatonic works well over the D7 chord, but if we play a major pentatonic a fifth higher (A major pentatonic) we might experience a clash between the note C# and the note C natural in the D7 chord. The "minor" pentatonic played a fifth higher however (A minor pentatonic), will outline the 5th, ♭7th, Root, 9th, and 11th, chord tones and extended chord tones over the D7 chord. Playing a major pentatonic a step higher than the Root D may also result in notes clashing with the chord tones. The minor pentatonic a step higher however (E minor pentatonic), will outline the 9th, 11th, 5th, 6th (or 13th), and root, chord tones and extended chord tones over the D7 chord (ex. 108). Example 109 shows a melodic line using the D major pentatonic along with the A minor and E minor pentatonics over a D7 chord.

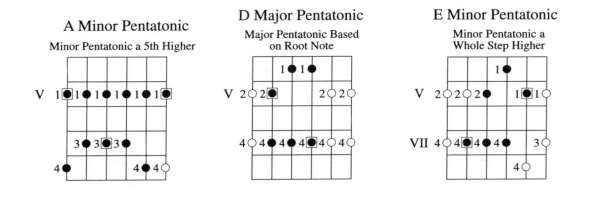

Ex. 108

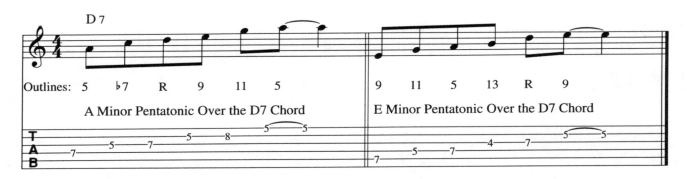

Ex. 109 - D Major Pentatonic Combined with the A Minor and E Minor Pentatonics Over D7

71

Example 110 shows triadic and scalar superimposing used along with the A blues scale and the A, D, and E Mixolydian modes.

Ex. 110

Blues Shuffle

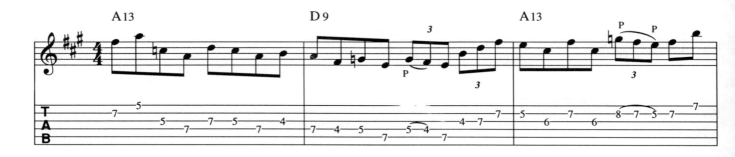

Soloing Over Chords With Extensions

Many of the chords in contemporary music have added tones which can be thought of as chord extensions or alterations that are based on the key the chord is in. As long as the added tones fall within the key the chord is in, you can improvise using the mode that is normally matched with the "seventh" form of the chord. The Ionian mode, for example, works with major 7 chords as well as major 9, major 13, major 6/9, major add 9, major sus4, and major sus2 chords that are I chords in a major key. The Dorian mode works with minor 7 as well as minor 9, minor 11 (also thought of as fourth chords), and minor 6 chords that are ii chords in a major key. The Mixolydian mode works with dominant 7 as well as dominant 9, dominant 11 and dominant 13 chords that are V chords in a major key.

In some instances, you will have chords that have extended tones that are not consistent with the key you're in. In some cases, you can think of the chord or chords as being in a "temporary" key for soloing purposes. This concept can be especially useful when you have successive minor 7 to dominant 7 chords (ii - V chords) with extended tones (ex. 111).

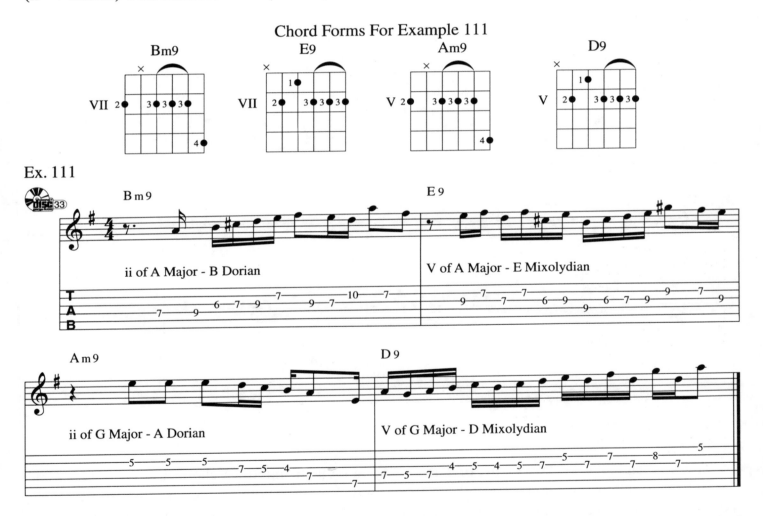

Ex. 111

The Mixolydian mode also works with dominant 7sus2 and dominant 7sus4 chords where the third of the chord has been replaced by the second or fourth degree of the Mixolydian mode. The dominant 7 sus4 chord is often interchangeable with a dominant 11 chord (a dominant 11 is often voiced so that it is essentially a IV triad over a V bass note - ex. 112). Many times you will see this chord as a secondary dominant or V chord in a "temporary" key and you would use a Mixolydian mode for soloing (ex. 113).

Ex. 112

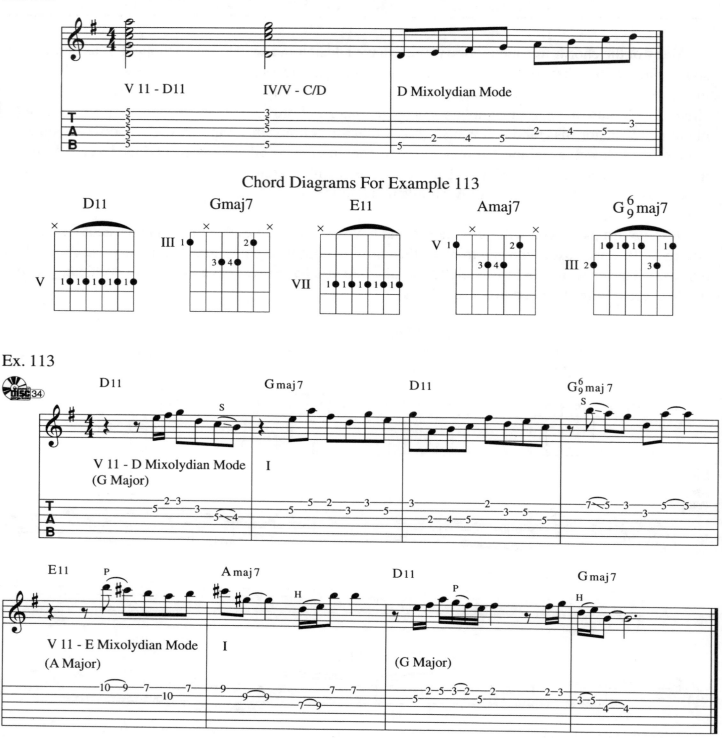

Chord Diagrams For Example 113

Ex. 113

The Aeolian mode works with minor 7 as well as minor 9 and minor 11 chords that are vi chords in a major key (or i chords in a minor key). The Aeolian mode isn't used with a minor 6th chord because there is a ♭6 interval on the 6th degree of the Aeolian mode, and a minor 6th chord has a major 6th interval (though the ♭6 is enharmonic to a ♯5 so the mode can be used with a minor 7♯5 chord).

The Phrygian mode works with minor 7 as well as minor 11 chords that are iii chords in a major key (ex. 114 - the Phrygian mode has a ♭9 interval and isn't used with minor 9 chords). Though the Phrygian mode (like the Aeolian mode) isn't used with a minor 6th chord (because there is a ♭6 interval on the 6th degree of the mode), it can be used with a minor 7♯5 chord (♭6 is enharmonic to ♯5) that is a iii

74

chord in a major key. Some interesting chord sequences can be made with the use of this chord while staying within the major key framework (ex. 115).

Chord Diagrams For Example 114

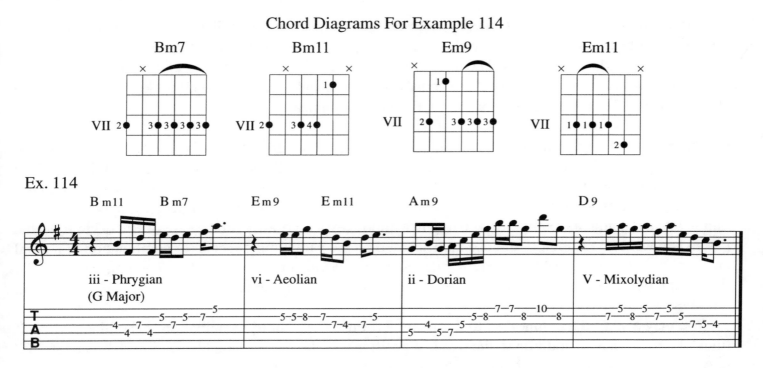

Ex. 114

iii - Phrygian
(G Major)

vi - Aeolian

ii - Dorian

V - Mixolydian

Chord Diagrams For Example 115

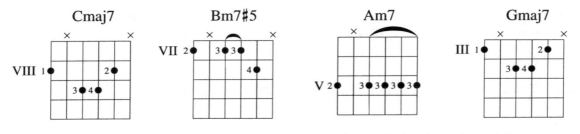

For the chord sequence based on A major play each chord two frets higher

Ex. 115

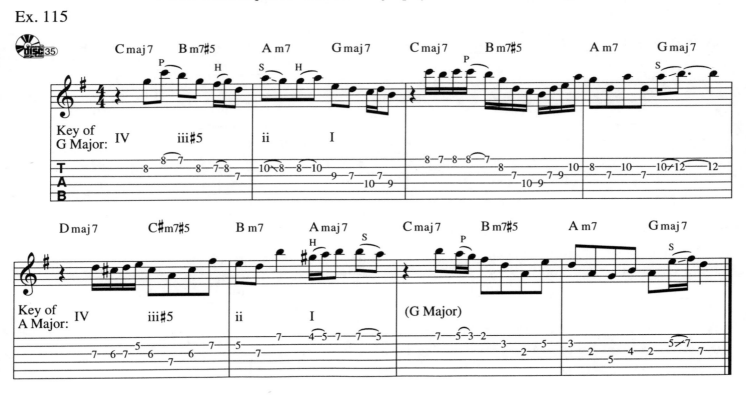

A Minor Key Approach to Altered Chords

Improvising over chords with altered notes can be one of the most challenging aspects of improvisation. This problem can often be simplified by using a minor key as a temporary key center for certain chord changes with altered notes. The minor7♭5 to dominant7♭9 chord sequence for example, is a common sequence in a minor key since these chords occur as ii and V chords in a minor key (the V7 or V7♭9 chord is built off of the 5th degree of the "harmonic" minor scale).

The minor7♭5 to dominant 7 (or dominant 7♭9) chord change will also be found in other musical situations besides being the ii and V chords in a minor key. Often, you will see the minor 7♭5 to dominant 7 combination replace the ii and V chords in a major key consequently resolving to a major chord. The progression Bm7♭5 to E7♭9 to Amaj7 would be an example of this. You can simply think of the minor 7♭5 and dominant7♭9 chords as being in a minor key temporarily (in the case of Bm7♭5 to E7♭9 the parent key would be A minor) and use modes based on the parent minor scale (or combination of natural and harmonic minor scales) to improvise over the minor 7♭5 to dominant 7 (or dom 7♭9) combination. For the I major chord (Amaj7) you would then use the Ionian mode or major scale (key of A major - ex. 116).

You may also find the minor7♭5 to dominant 7 (or dom7♭9) chord combination in the iii and vi positions of a major key in addition to the ii and V positions. In the progression C♯m7♭5 - F♯7 - Bm7♭5 - E7 to A maj7, you can think of each minor7♭5 to dominant 7 combination as being the ii m7♭5 and V 7 chords in their own temporary minor key center. The C♯m7♭5 to F♯7 would be the ii m7♭5 and V 7 from the key of B minor, while the Bm7♭5 and E7 chords would be the ii m7♭5 and V 7 from the key of A minor. These chords would then resolve to A maj7 which is of course, the I chord in the key of A major (ex. 117).

Chord Diagrams for Examples 116 thru 120

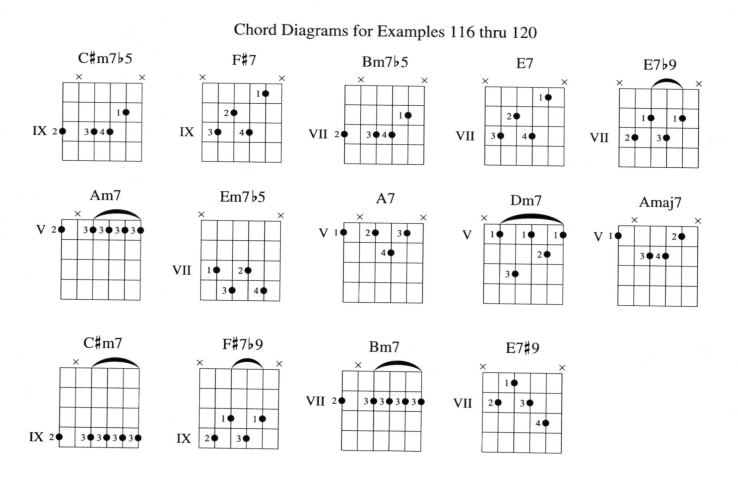

76

Scale Fingerings for Examples 116, 117 and 118

● = Root   O = Additional scale notes above or below the root notes.

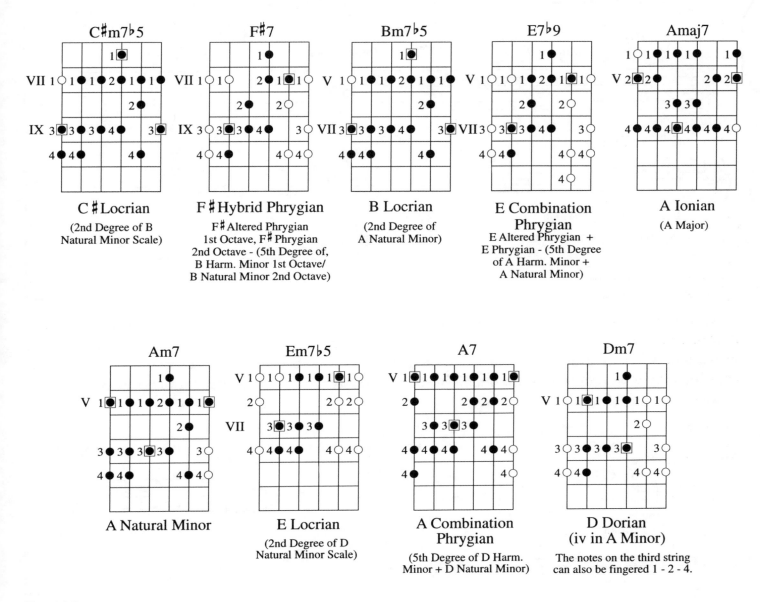

C♯ Locrian
(2nd Degree of B Natural Minor Scale)

F♯ Hybrid Phrygian
F♯ Altered Phrygian 1st Octave, F♯ Phrygian 2nd Octave - (5th Degree of, B Harm. Minor 1st Octave/ B Natural Minor 2nd Octave)

B Locrian
(2nd Degree of A Natural Minor)

E Combination Phrygian
E Altered Phrygian + E Phrygian - (5th Degree of A Harm. Minor + A Natural Minor)

A Ionian
(A Major)

A Natural Minor

E Locrian
(2nd Degree of D Natural Minor Scale)

A Combination Phrygian
(5th Degree of D Harm. Minor + D Natural Minor)

D Dorian
(iv in A Minor)
The notes on the third string can also be fingered 1 - 2 - 4.

Ex. 116

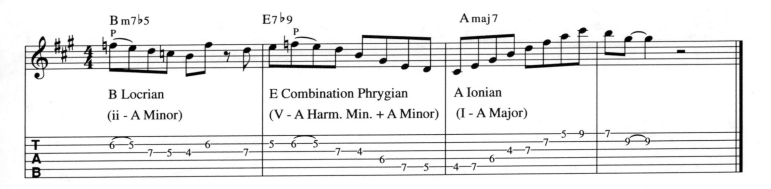

B Locrian
(ii - A Minor)

E Combination Phrygian
(V - A Harm. Min. + A Minor)

A Ionian
(I - A Major)

Ex. 117

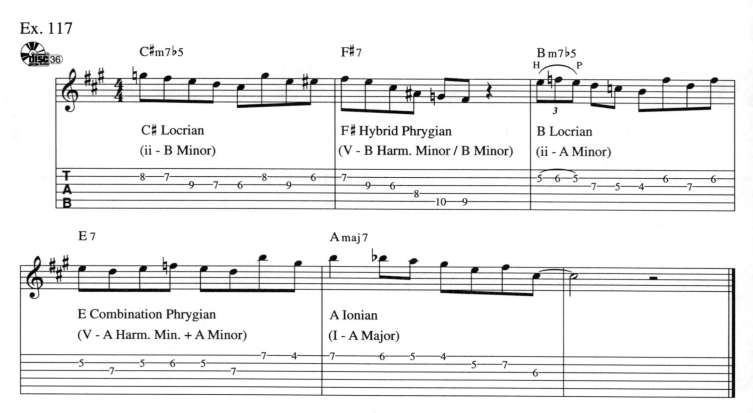

In example 118 you can view the chords Em7b5 to A7 as being the ii m7b5 and V 7 of D minor (temporary key). The D minor 7 chord in measure five functions as the iv chord in A minor, though it might also be thought of as the i in D minor (temporary key) because of the chords that precede it in measure four. The progression eventually resolves to an A minor chord after a Bm7b5 to E7 chord sequence (the ii m7b5 and V7 in A minor).

Ex. 118

Example 119 shows the "mixing" of temporary major and minor key centers for minor 7 (regular 5th) to altered dominant chord changes. In this case the C#m7 can be thought of as the ii chord from B major, however the F#7b9 would be the V chord in B minor. The Bm7 chord is the ii in A major while the E7b9 is the V chord from A minor which finally resolves to an A maj7 chord (the I chord in the key of A major).

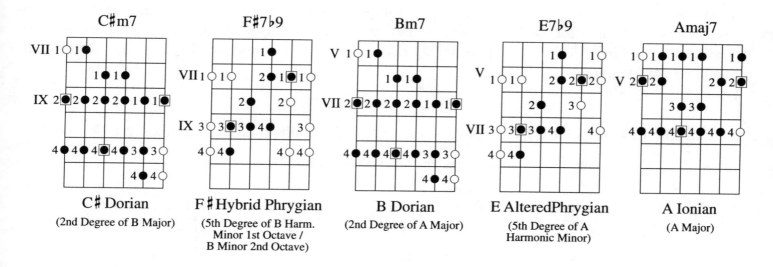

Ex. 119

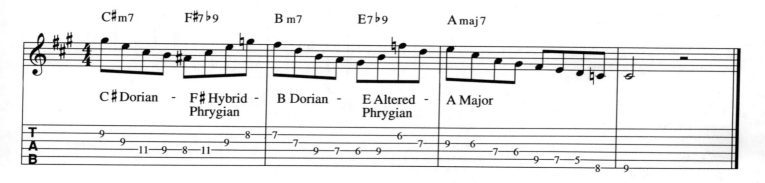

Sometimes you will encounter altered dominant chords that aren't preceded by minor 7 or minor 7b5 chords (or ii chords). Scales that are based on the "5th" degree of either the harmonic minor scale or a combination of the harmonic minor and natural minor scales can be used for improvising over many types of altered dominant chords as well as dominant 7th chords that are not altered (whether they function as V chords or not).

The altered phrygian scale (5th degree of the harmonic minor scale) can work with dominant 7, domi-nant 7♭9, dominant 7♯5, and dominant 7♯5♭9 chords. The combination Phrygian (5th degree of harmonic minor plus natural minor) and hybrid Phrygian (5th degree of harmonic minor for the 1st octave, 5th degree of natural minor for the 2nd octave) are particularly useful scales because they can be played over dominant 7, dominant 7♭9, and dominant 7♯9 chords as well as dominant 7♯5, dominant 7♯5♭9, and dominant 7♯5♯9 chords.

Example 120 shows the E hybrid phrygian scale mixed with the E blues scale over an E7♯9 chord.

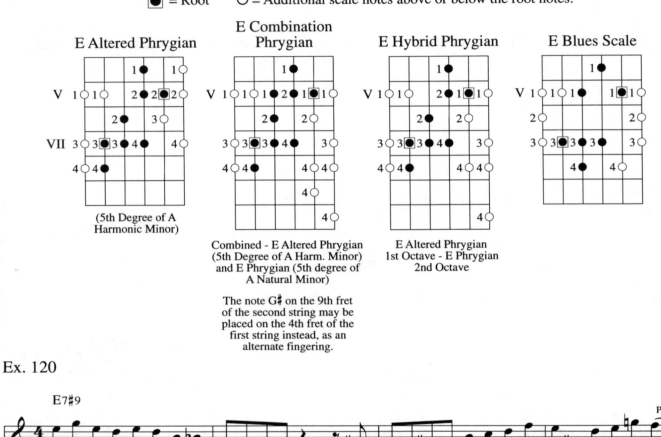

Ex. 120

Mixing Keys

We have seen the use of mixing keys where a ii m7♭5 to V 7 chord sequence from a minor key resolves to a I maj7 chord or the I chord from the parallel major key. A major key may have chords "borrowed" from the parallel minor key (same root name) for chord progressions that don't fit within the usual sequence of chords built from a major key. For example, you might see a iii - vi - IV - iv minor - I maj7 chord sequence. While all of the other chords fit in the major key, the iv minor chord could be thought of as being borrowed from the minor key with the same root name (parallel minor) as the major key. Since the key of A major has a Dmaj7 as the IV chord, in order to solo over a Dm7 chord (put into the iv position) we can think of that chord as being borrowed from the key of A minor which has a minor 7 chord built on the fourth degree (ex. 121).

Ex. 121 - Jazz Rock Slow 4

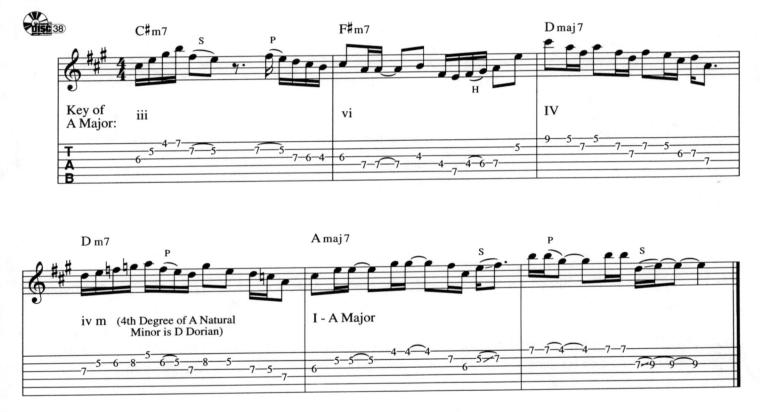

The concept of "mixing" keys or scales can be useful along with the temporary key concept that covers minor 7 to dominant 7 chord combinations or minor 7♭5 to altered dominant combinations. Example 122 illustrates the use of these concepts combined.

Ex. 122

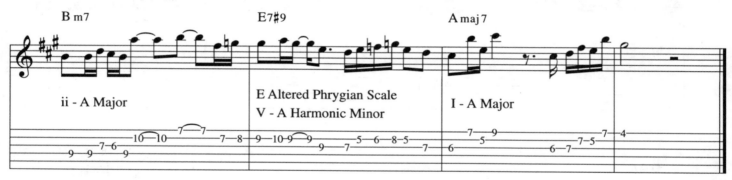

Example 123 has a chord progression which is based on the key of A major that has dominant 7th chords (C#7, F#7, and B7) that don't fit within the group of chords that are built on those roots in the key of A major (normally C#m7 - iii, F#m7 - vi, Bm7 - ii). These dominant 7th chords can be thought of as individual "V" chords or secondary dominants (root a fifth above the root of the chord that follows). A Mixolydian mode can be used with each of the dominant 7th chords (un-altered) in example 123.

Scale Forms for Example 123

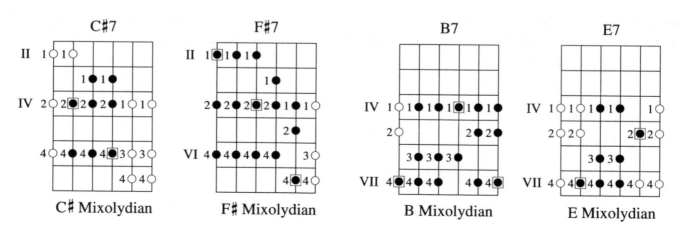

82

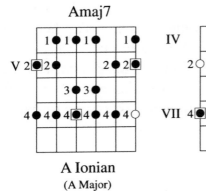

Amaj7

A Ionian

(A Major)

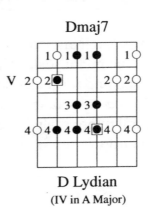

Bm7

B Dorian

(ii in A Major)

Dmaj7

D Lydian

(IV in A Major)

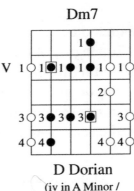

Dm7

D Dorian

(iv in A Minor /
also ii in C Major)

The notes on the third string can
also be fingered 1 - 2 - 4.

Ex. 123

The Melodic Minor Scale

The melodic minor scale was originally conceived to compensate for the 1 1/2 step skip between the 6th and 7th degree of the harmonic minor scale. The melodic minor scale has traditionally had ascending and descending forms. The ascending form can be thought of as a natural minor scale with raised sixth and seventh degrees. It can also be viewed as a major scale with a flat 3rd. The descending form of the melodic minor scale is the natural minor scale intact. In contemporary soloing the ascending form is used whether the scale is played up or down (ex. 124).

Ex. 124 - Melodic Minor Scale - Jazz Form

Melodic Minor Scale Fingerings - Five Positions

● = Root   O = Additional scale notes above or below the root notes.

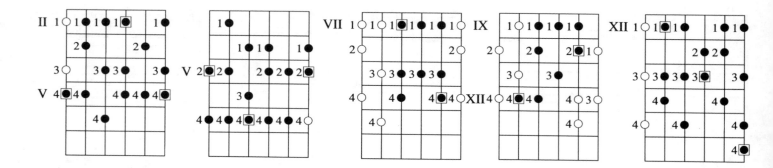

The melodic minor scale can be used for minor chords, minor 6th chords, and minor chords with a major 7th added (ex. 125). The minor M7 chord is often used as a passing chord in a minor, min M7, min 7, min 6 chord progression. With a chord sequence like this you can use the arpeggios related to the chords when soloing to develop a melodic sequence (ex. 126). The arpeggio derived from the melodic minor scale is a minor triad with a major 7th (R, ♭3, 5, maj7) and by mixing extensions with the lower chord tones some interesting melodic lines can be created (ex. 127). Example 128 shows some melodic ideas that alternate the natural minor scale for the minor 7 chord with the melodic minor scale for a minor 6th chord.

Ex. 125

Ex. 126

Ex. 127

Ex. 128

85

The Diminished Scale

The Diminished scale (whole-half form) is made up of alternating whole and half steps (ex. 129). There are 9 notes in the scale including the repeat of the root note (it is sometimes called an 8 tone scale because there are 8 "different" tones). It is used with diminished chords (using dim. 7 or °7 symbols) and can also be used for altered dominant chords by playing the scale half-step, whole-step (which is discussed later). The arpeggio is derived by playing the 1st, 3rd, 5th and 7th notes of the whole-half scale form and has intervals R, ♭3, ♭5 and ♭♭7 (enharmonic to a 6th).

Ex. 129

The diminished arpeggio is made up of repeating ♭3rd intervals, and both the scale shapes and arpeggio shapes will invert symmetrically (retaining their shape and fingering) every ♭3rd interval. That means that the C diminished scale and arpeggio will have the same shape and fingering as the A diminished scale and arpeggio (but started from the note C). Consequently the E♭ diminished scale and arpeggio will have the same shape and fingering as the C diminished scale and arpeggio (this time started from E♭) and so on (fig. Q).

Figure Q

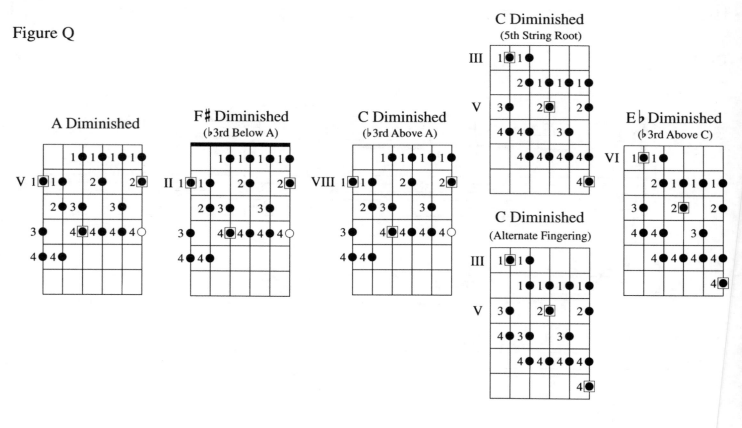

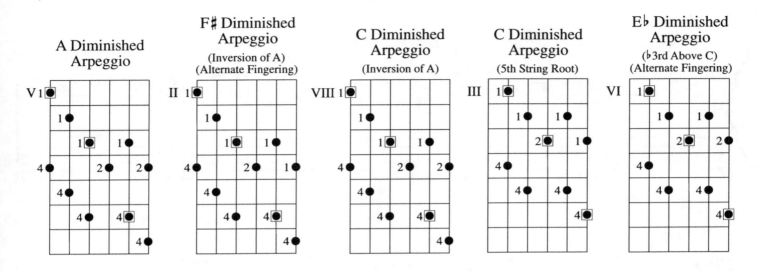

A Diminished
Arpeggio

F♯ Diminished
Arpeggio
(Inversion of A)
(Alternate Fingering)

C Diminished
Arpeggio
(Inversion of A)

C Diminished
Arpeggio
(5th String Root)

E♭ Diminished
Arpeggio
(♭3rd Above C)
(Alternate Fingering)

Because of the shapes inverting symmetrically every ♭3rd interval, some interesting vertical patterns can be derived (ex. 130).

Vertically Inverted Patterns

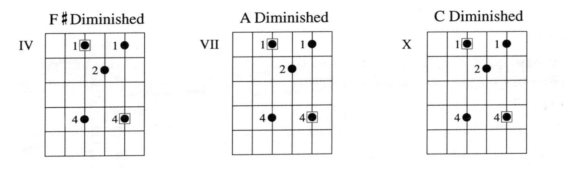

F♯ Diminished

A Diminished

C Diminished

Ex. 130

(The note G♭ is enharmonic to F♯)

Diminished Chord Shapes

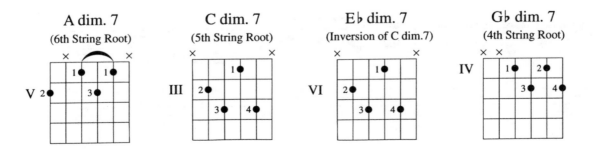

A dim. 7
(6th String Root)

C dim. 7
(5th String Root)

E♭ dim. 7
(Inversion of C dim.7)

G♭ dim. 7
(4th String Root)

Examples 131 through 135 show musical ideas using the A diminished scale and arpeggio.

Ex. 131

Ex. 132

Ex. 133

Ex. 134

Ex. 135

The Half–Whole Diminished Scale

The half-whole form of the diminished scale (also called the 8 tone dominant scale) is used to improvise over altered dominant chords that have a ♭9, ♯9, ♭5 (♯11), 13th, or a combination of these notes. The scale can simply be thought of as a regular diminished scale (whole-half) started a half step lower. For example, the A half-whole diminished scale has the same notes as the B♭ whole-half diminished scale because of the continual alternation of half steps and whole steps in both scales. The half-whole diminished scale is especially effective over dominant 7♭9 chords. Note in example 136 that the A7♭9 chord can be viewed as a B♭ diminished 7th chord over an A root.

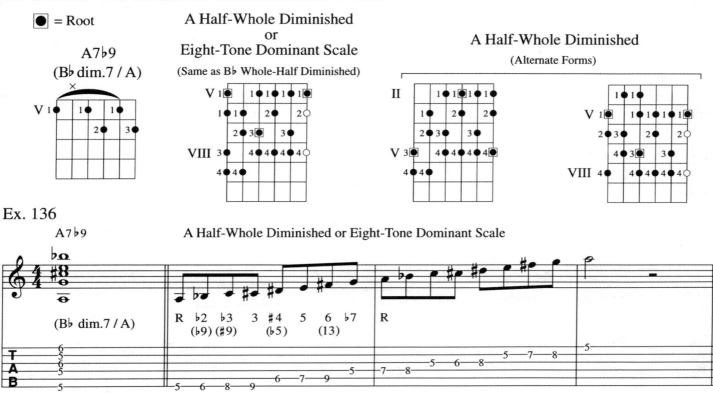

Ex. 136

A diminished arpeggio can be built by using the 3rd, 5th, ♭7th, and ♭9th of a dominant 7♭9 chord. Because the distance between these notes is a ♭3rd interval (remember the diminished arpeggio inverts every ♭3rd interval), a diminished arpeggio can be built off of any of these degrees (ex. 137).

Ex. 137

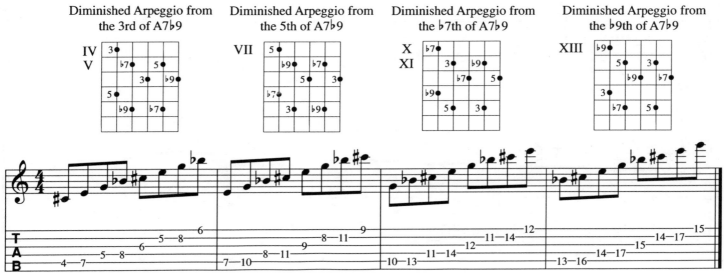

Examples 138 through 142 show melodic ideas that incorporate the diminished arpeggio and the half-whole diminished scale (Eight-Tone Dominant).

Ex. 138

Ex. 139

Ex. 140

Ex. 141

Ex. 142

The Whole Tone Scale

The whole tone scale is a scale that is made up of successive whole steps (ex. 143).

A Whole Tone Scale

● = Root

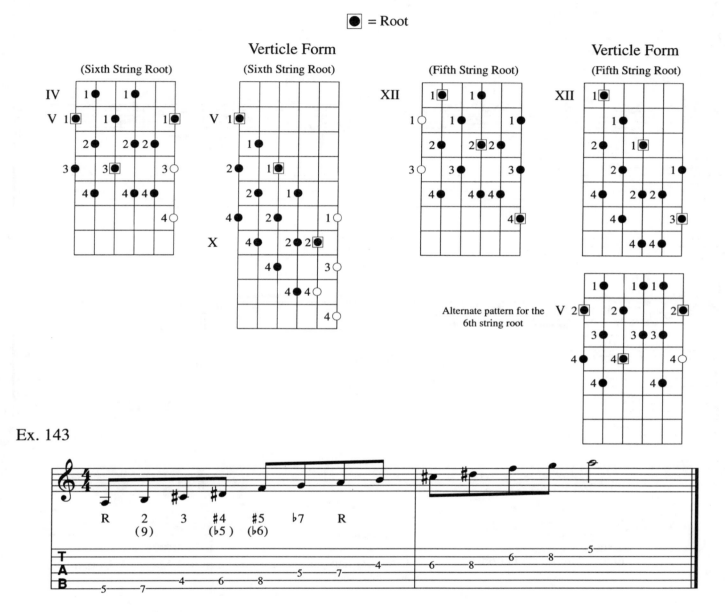

Ex. 143

The whole tone scale is primarily used for improvising over augmented chords and dominant 7th chords where the 5th has been altered (♭5 or ♯5) but the 9th is not altered. It can also be used for dominant 7th chords whose alterations are enharmonic to a ♭5 or ♯5 (♯11 or ♭13) with the 9th remaining unaltered. Examples 144 and 145 illustrate the whole tone scale being played over a dominant 7♭5 chord in a Jazz progression.

You will often find dominant 7♭5 chords as tri-tone substitutes for "V" altered dominant chords (a tri-tone is the interval of a flat 5th). This type of chord substitution provides chromatic movement in the bass, and the whole tone scale can produce interesting melodic tension before resolving to the I chord (ex. 145). When there is chromatic movement in the bass but the chord is not a dominant 7♭5 (2nd measure of ex. 146), you would use the scale that is appropriate to the chord type.

Ex. 144

Ex. 145

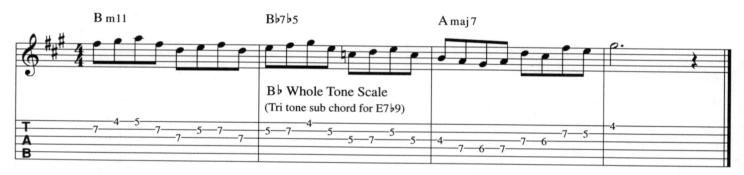

Ex. 146

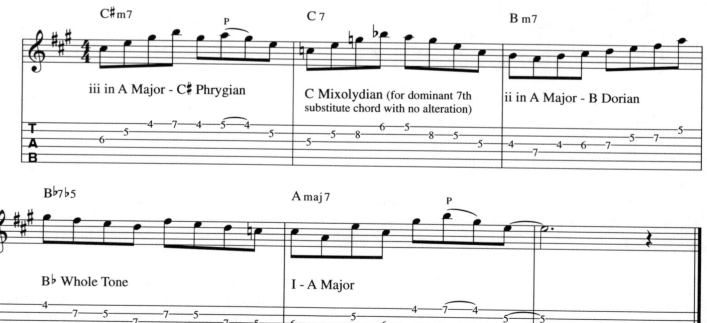

Combinations Using Whole Tone And Diminished Scales

Scales can also be constructed by combining elements of the whole tone and diminished scales. A scale known as the overtone dominant scale (also known as the Lydian ♭7 scale, which is the fourth "mode" of the melodic minor scale) can be viewed as a combination of the whole tone and diminished (half-whole form) scales (ex. 147). This scale is similar to the Mixolydian mode but has a raised 4th (♯11) degree. This scale is useful over dominant chords where the 5th is flatted, dominant 7♯11 chords, and can be superimposed over dominant chords that have no alteration. By reversing this pattern, we can create a scale by using diminished (half-whole) scale notes with whole tone scale notes (ex. 148). This scale (also known as the super Locrian which is the 7th mode of the melodic minor scale), is particularly useful because it works with dominant chords where the 5th and / or 9th has been altered. Examples 149 and 150 show melodic lines using both of these scales.

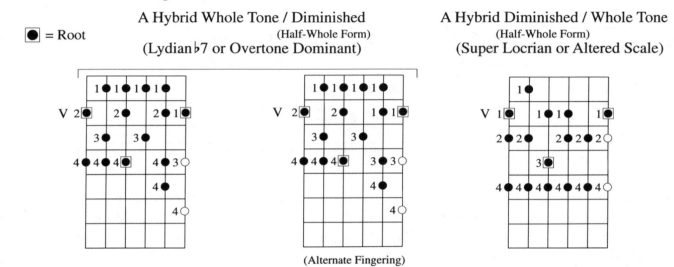

Ex. 147 - A Hybrid Whole Tone / Diminished - also known as the Overtone Dominant or Lydian ♭7 Scale
(Half-Whole Form)

Ex. 148 - A Hybrid Diminished / Whole Tone - also known as the Super Locrian or Altered Scale
(Half-Whole Form)

Ex. 149

A7♭5

A Hybrid Whole Tone / Diminished - (Lydian ♭7 or Overtone Dominant)
(Half-Whole form)

Ex. 150

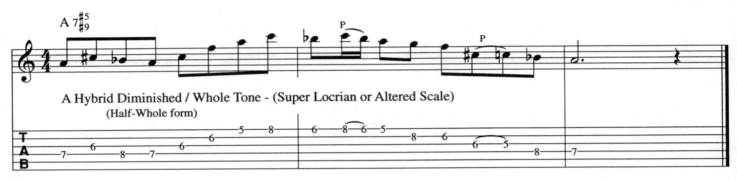

A 7♯5♯9

A Hybrid Diminished / Whole Tone - (Super Locrian or Altered Scale)
(Half-Whole form)

By combining the "whole-half" form of the diminished scale with the whole tone scale, two additional scales can be constructed. The hybrid whole tone / diminished scale using the whole-half form of the diminished scale, is also known as the Lydian augmented scale (which is the third mode of the melodic minor scale). This scale can be used for maj7♯11 and maj7♯5 chords (ex. 151). The hybrid diminished / whole tone scale using the whole-half form of the diminished scale, is also known as the Locrian natural 2 scale (which is the sixth mode of the melodic minor scale). This scale works with minor 7♭5 and minor 9♭5 chords (ex. 152). Examples 153 and 154 show solo lines created from these scales.

A Hybrid Whole Tone / Diminished
(Whole-Half Form)
(Lydian Augmented Scale)

A Hybrid Diminished / Whole Tone
(Whole-Half Form)
(Locrian Natural 2 Scale)

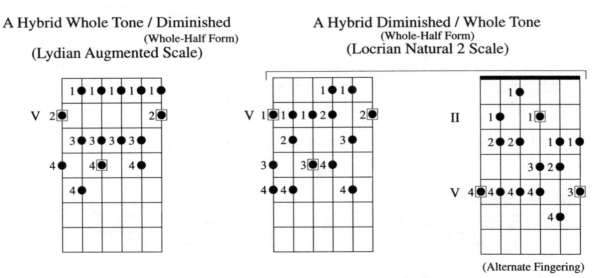

(Alternate Fingering)

The 1st finger can be used instead of the 2nd finger on the first string along with the 2nd finger being used instead of the 3rd finger on the second string as an alternate fingering.

Ex. 151 - A Hybrid Whole Tone / Diminished - also known as the Lydian Augmented Scale
(Whole-Half form)

Ex. 152 - A Hybrid Diminished / Whole Tone - also known as the Locrian Natural 2 Scale
(Whole-Half form)

Ex. 153

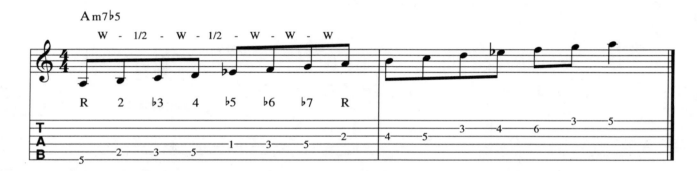

A Hybrid Whole Tone / Diminished - (Lydian Augmented)
(Whole-Half form)

Ex. 154

A Hybrid Diminished / Whole Tone - (Locrian Natural 2)
(Whole-Half form)

Combining Elements

Now that we have explored some ways of approaching different chord types we should look at how the soloing elements fit together in a chord progression. Example 155 uses a combination of the elements that have been presented. Notice in this example that the E major scale is the parent scale (the scale that the modes were built from) in a number of cases. This can provide a common thread which you can build on.

Ex. 155

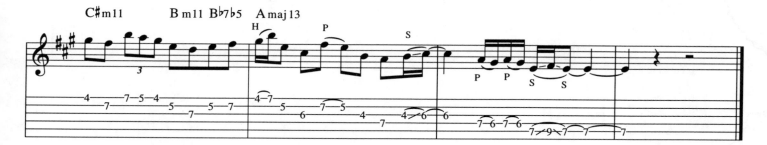

Explanation of Soloing Elements used in Example 155

Chord

Amaj13   –   Superimposed A Lydian mode (4th degree of E major) as well as the B, E, and A major pentatonics and the A major extended arpeggio

D#m7b5   –   D# Locrian mode (7th degree of E major / also 2nd degree of C# natural minor)

G#7#5#9   –   G# hybrid Phrygian and the G#7#5#9 arpeggio

F#m9   –   F# Dorian mode (2nd degree of E major)

B13   –   B Mixolydian mode (5th degree of E major) and superimposed B Blues / Dorian combination scale

B7b9   –   B hybrid Phrygian scale

Emaj7   –   E Ionian mode (major scale) and superimposing using the E major extended arpeggio (based on the E major scale)

Bb7b5   –   Bb whole tone scale

C#m11   –   C# natural minor scale (6th degree of E major)

Bm11   –   B Dorian mode (2nd degree of A major)

Appendix I - Mode-Arpeggio Guide

(Based on the Key of G Major)

● = Root   ○ = Additional mode or arpeggio notes above or below the root.

Numbers by arpeggio notes refer to the interval from the root.

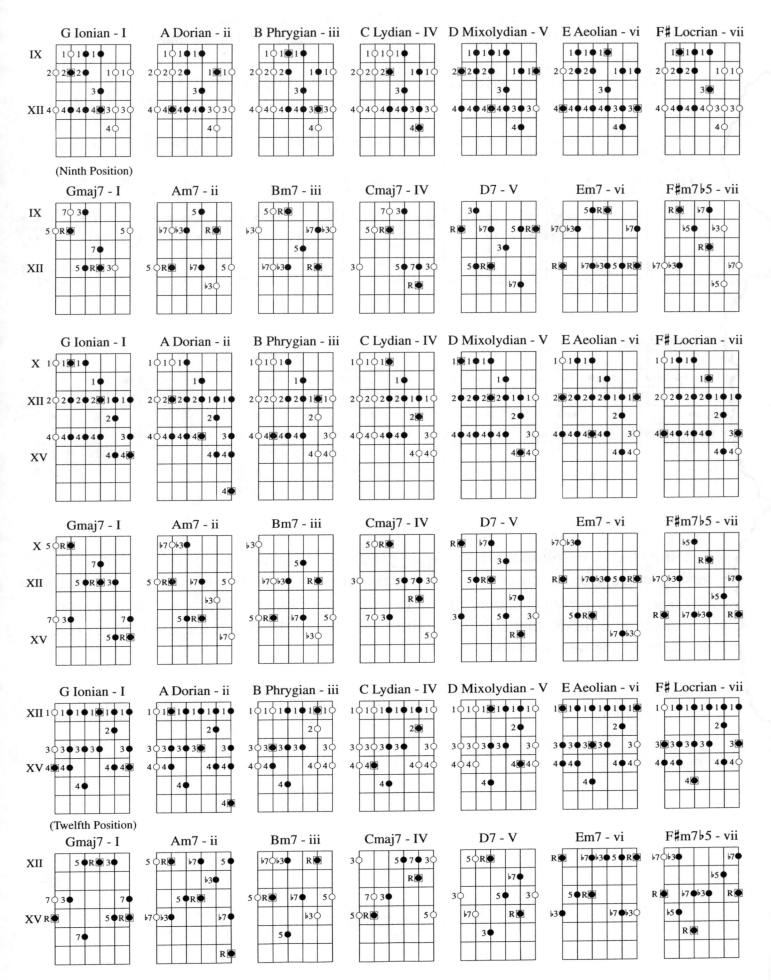

99

Alternate patterns for the 12th position forms
(the note F♯ has been placed on the third string instead of the fourth)

The notes on the third string can be fingered 1 - 1 - 3 instead of 1 - 2 - 4 to accomodate different note patterns

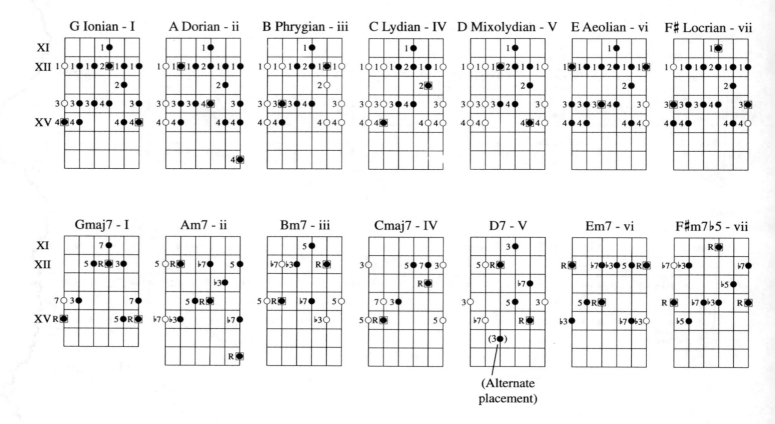

(Alternate placement)

It is important to explore scale and arpeggio patterns throughout the fingerboard. Though these shapes are presented in the key of G major, it is important to practice them in different keys. These are moveable shapes, so you can play any mode from any root note by moving the root note of a mode shape to the desired location of the new root note and playing the mode shape in the new location.

Appendix II – Scale – Chord Relationships

SCALE	INTERVALS	ASSOCIATED CHORD TYPES
Ionian	R 2 3 4 5 6 7 R (9) (11) (13)	Major, Maj7, Maj9, Maj6, Maj6/9, Maj sus4, 6/9 maj7 Maj sus2, Maj add6, Maj add9
Dorian	R 2 ♭3 4 5 6 ♭7 R	minor, min7, min9, min6, min11, minor 13, minor 7 sus2, min 7 sus4
Phrygian	R ♭2 ♭3 4 5 ♭6 ♭7 R	minor, min7, min7#5, min7#5♭9, min11
Lydian	R 2 3 #4 5 6 7 R	Major, Maj7, Maj9, Maj7#11, Maj9#11, Maj7♭5
Mixolydian	R 2 3 4 5 6 ♭7 R	Dominant 7, Major, Dom 9, Dom11, Dom 13, Dom7sus4, Dom9sus4, Dom7sus2, Maj add6, Maj add9, Major sus4, Major sus2
Aeolian (Natural Minor)	R 2 ♭3 4 5 ♭6 ♭7 R	minor, minor7, min9, min11
Locrian	R ♭2 ♭3 4 ♭5 ♭6 ♭7 R	minor7♭5, minor7#5, min7#5♭9, minor 7♭5 13, min7♭5♭9
Harmonic Minor	R 2 ♭3 4 5 ♭6 7 R	minor, minor add9, min (maj7)

Altered Phrygian
(Spanish Phrygian)
	R ♭2 3 4 5 ♭6 ♭7 R
	(♭9) (#5)
	                      or
	                      (♭13)
		Dominant 7, Dom7♭9, Dom7#5,
		Dom7#5♭9, Dom7sus4, Major,
		Maj sus4

Combination Phrygian	R ♭2 ♭3 - 3 4 5 ♭6 ♭7 R
	(♭9)(#9) (#5)
	                              or
	                              (♭13)
		Dominant 7, Dom7♭9, Dom7#9,
		Dom7#5, Dom7#5♭9, Dom7#5#9,
		Dom7♭13, Dom7♭13(♭9 or #9),
		Dom7 sus4, Major, Major sus4

Hybrid Phrygian	R ♭2 3 4 5 ♭6 ♭7 (1st Octave)
	R ♭2 ♭3 4 5 ♭6 ♭7 R (2nd Octave)
	(♭9)(#9) (#5)
	                              or
	                              (♭13)
		Same as
		Combination Phrygian

SCALE	INTERVALS	ASSOCIATED CHORD TYPES
Melodic Minor	R 2 b3 4 5 6 7 R	minor, minor 6, minor maj 7, min add9
Diminished (Whole-Half)	R 2 b3 4 b5 b6 6 7 R (#5) (bb7)	Dim. 7, Dim. 9, Dim. 7b13
Half-Whole Diminished (Eight Tone Dominant)	R b2 b3 - 3 #4 5 6 b7 R (b9)(#9) (#11) (b5)	Dominant 7, Dom7b5, Dom7#11 Dom 7#9, Dom7b9, Dom7b5b9, Dom7b5 #9, Dom13b9
Whole Tone	R 2 3 #4 #5 b7 R (b5) (b6)	Major #5 (augmented), Dom7#5, Dom7b5, Dom7#11, Dom9#11
Hybrid Whole Tone / Diminished (Half-Whole) (Overtone Dominant / Lydian b7)	R 2 3 #4 5 6 b7 R (#11) (b5)	Dominant 7, Dom9, Dom13, Dom7b5, Dom7#11, Dom9#11
Hybrid Diminished / Whole Tone (Half-Whole) (Super Locrian / Altered Scale)	R b2 b3 3 b5 b6 b7 R (b9)(#9) (b4)(#11)(#5)	Dom7b5, Dom7#5, Dom7b5b9, Dom7b5#9, Dom7#5b9 Dom7#5#9, Dom7b5b13
Hybrid Whole Tone / Diminished (Whole-Half) (Lydian Augmented)	R 2 3 #4 #5 6 7 R (#11)	Major #5 (augmented), Maj7#5, Maj7b5, and Maj7#11, Maj9#11, Maj13#11 (where the 5th is omit- ted or replaced by the #11)
Hybrid Diminished / Whole Tone (Whole-Half) (Locrian Natural 2)	R 2 b3 4 b5 b6 b7 R (#5)	minor7b5, min9b5, min7#5

Progressing Onward

   By practicing the ideas in this method in other keys and exploring all areas of the fingerboard, you will find improvising to be a constantly evolving experience. Each new musical idea you develop will interact with others and ultimately grow and expand into more musical ideas. Being aware of all of the elements of music can help your creativity and make you a better musician as well as a better soloist.

About The Author

Scott Reed graduated from the University of Southern California and received a Bachelors Degree in Music Performance with a major in Studio Guitar. He is a two-time recipient of a music fellowship from the National Endowment for the Arts and has taught applied guitar for Governors State University. In addition to doing studio work he has played countless shows and concerts throughout the United States.

EXCELLENCE IN MUSIC